EMPATH DEVELOPMENT

A Spiritual and Emotional Guide for Your
Healing and Growth

PANAGIOTIS PAPADOPOULOS

Table of Contents

Introduction

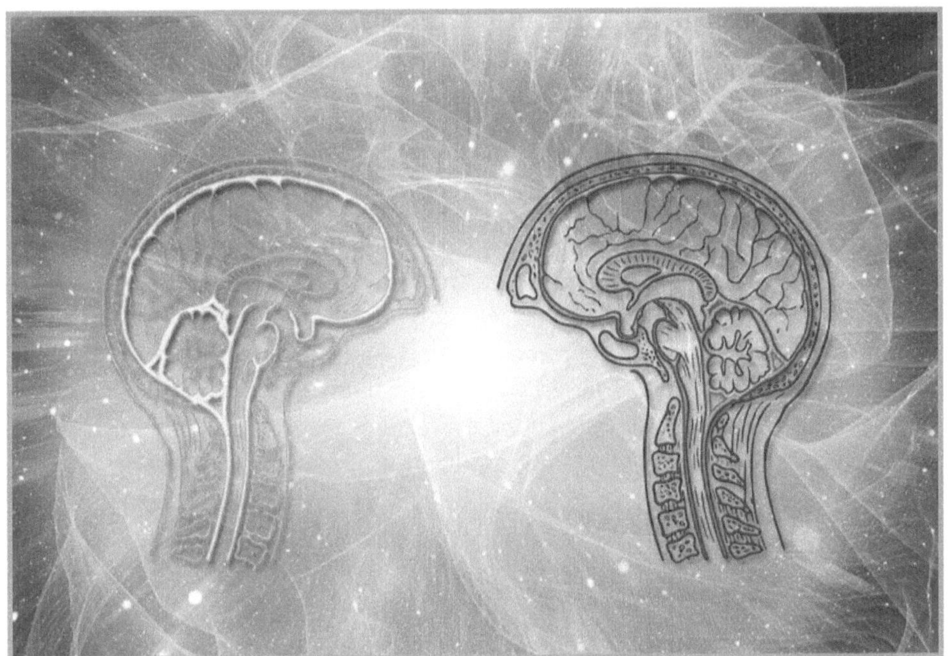

Have you ever felt like you were understanding to a fault? Does the thought of other people crying always make you cry, regardless of what it's about? Do you enjoy spending time with other people but find yourself feeling overwhelmed or drained after social interactions? Would you consider yourself an introvert? If this is relatable to you, then you may be what is known as an empath. In this book, we will explore what it means to be an empath, how this is a gift, and how you can further develop this talent.

If you are reading this book, you probably either identify as an empath or think you might be a highly sensitive individual. If you're not familiar with either of these terms, you may just be looking to become more in tune with yourself, your surroundings, and how you relate to other people. The term "empath" has recently become relevant to popular culture, as more people are becoming aware of how they might relate to this personality type. In an age of social media, it is hard not to become consumed with the feelings and emotions of others. If you consistently check your twitter to see news headlines about all the tragedies going on in the world, you may find yourself a bit overwhelmed. This is understandable, as constant stimulation, especially emotionally-charged stimulation, can be draining and overwhelming.

It is extremely common for empaths to experience this, as they are consistently taking in other people's emotions, and more and more people are identifying as empaths as we adjust to a stimulating culture of emotions being expressed online and on social media. It can seem impossible to escape this, simply because we are surrounded by emotions being thrown at us every time we open our phones or turn on the news. However, identifying as an empath is not necessarily a negative thing. In fact, it can often be considered a gift. With the right understanding and self-care tools, you can develop this gift and excel socially as an empath.

An empath is broadly defined as a person who is able to internalize the emotions of other people around them. The term obviously relates to the concept of empathy, which is defined as the ability to understand and even feel other people's emotions. While humans are generally able to experience empathy, such as feeling sad for a friend when they lose a loved one, being an empath is rarer. Empaths experience this sensation to the point where they are unable to control it and can experience the emotions of other people almost to the same degree.

While the two terms are connected, it is important to distinguish that merely experiencing empathy does not make a person an empath. Empaths identify as people who experience a lot of empathy all the time, sometimes to the point where they feel drained or overwhelmed (Orloff, 2017). They frequently find themselves overstimulated and unable to block out certain stimuli the way that others can. There are different psychological characteristics that go into being an empath, which we will explore in later chapters. Simply put, however, empaths process emotions and energy differently due to their hypersensitive neurons (Orloff, 2017).

Empaths And Spirituality

Being an empath is also often connected to different forms of spirituality. As developed in the science fiction world, being an empath is seen as a sort of superpower. Many people believe that empaths are much more in tune with and able to internalize the emotions and energy of other people, which can pair well with energy healing or other practices that require a deep understanding of another person's emotions. Some even believe that being an empath can be a sign of having psychic abilities. Empaths have an extremely strong sense of other people's energies, making them good spiritual healers and clairvoyants.

According to psychiatrist Judith Orloff, who has conducted extensive research about the psychiatry behind empathy and identifies as an empath herself, empaths are often very sensitive to the energy that flows within and without humans. Empaths are also able to experience high levels of intuition, although these gifts are not often encouraged and can be suppressed in childhood and early adulthood (Mason, 2005). In later chapters, we will explore how to develop intuitive gifts that have been suppressed, and how to become more aware of the way that our brains are able to pick up on other people's energies. Furthermore, even non-empaths can train themselves to become more empathetic and sensitive to other people's emotions and energies, which can allow us to develop some of these skills even if they do not come quite as naturally.

Are You An Empath?

As mentioned earlier, you probably chose this book because you suspect you may be an empath. You may also be interested in the energetics behind empathy and want to learn more about how you can develop your gifts of intuition. In the next few chapters, we will delve into what makes a person an empath, how to develop and use your empathy while avoiding burnout, and how a person's empathy can connect to different spiritual practices.

Even if you don't fully identify as an empath, you may consider yourself to be a Highly Sensitive Person (HSP). HSPs often exhibit a lot of the same qualities as empaths, as certain functions of the brain work the same way in both types of person. If this is the case for you, this book will still be helpful in allowing you to develop your empathy while still being able to avoid the burnout that can come with being highly sensitive. If you are still confused about whether you are an empath, that's okay. We will further explore what being an empath means and how it affects your life in these next few chapters. And if you aren't totally convinced that you are an empath, that's fine too! Empathy is an emotion that can be developed further, and you can still use it as a tool to move forward in your own forms of spirituality.

01

CHAPTER

What Makes An Empath?

➤ Common Qualities of Empaths

One of the main characteristics of an empath is sensitivity, in its traditional sense. Empaths have highly sensitive neurological functions, causing them to experience high levels of stimulation. While most people are able to filter out stimulation and instead choose what they want to focus on, empaths are unable to do so (Orloff, 2018). They essentially feel everything, picking up on all the energies around them. Because of this, empaths can become overstimulated and overwhelmed very quickly. This can also make them very susceptible to emotional contagion, which can often occur in large groups. Even non-empaths can experience this phenomenon. Have you ever noticed how someone being particularly on-edge around you can make you irritable or anxious as well? But for empaths, this is an even more extreme phenomenon and something that is very difficult to filter out. This is just another reason why empaths usually need to spend time alone in order to recharge and ground themselves. As we will discuss in this chapter, many characteristics of being an empath are things that occur among non-empaths, just in a much more heightened form.

In short, empaths and Highly Sensitive People are different from people who do not identify with these categories because of the way their brains work. Empaths and HSPs have hyper-sensitive neurons that cause them to internalize the pain and emotions of other people, often to the same degree. However, they are not necessarily aware of the phenomenon that is happening in their brain that causes them to do this. Furthermore, while empaths share all the qualities of HSPs, they take these qualities further by being able to pick up on people's subtle energies and internalize them. Because of this important distinction, we will be focusing not only on the everyday aspects of being an empath, but also the specific spiritual processes that empaths are often able to perform. Later in this chapter, we will explore the functions happening in our brains that allow us to feel empathy. However, let's first explore how these functions manifest themselves in our behaviors and emotions so that we can explore the common qualities of empaths.

Since the concept of being an empath is a relatively newer idea, we can discuss empathy as it relates to other aspects of a person's personality. One scale commonly used to assess personality is the Big Five scale. The traits measured on this scale are openness, conscientiousness, extraversion, agreeableness, and neuroticism. These traits are often brought up as they relate to empaths and the concept of empathy, though the presence of empathy in a person can vary. However, it is often found that people who identify as empaths also have high levels of conscientiousness, and those who have disorders characterized by low empathy levels generally have lower levels of conscientiousness. As we explore what it means to be an empath, we will discuss the different ways that the common traits make up a person's personality.

Common Qualities Of Empaths

Orloff, who has done extensive research on empaths, has developed a short list with some common traits of empaths to help people determine if they identify as an empath. We will discuss some of these traits in detail to help you determine if you are an empath, or if you have some of the traits of an empath that you could develop. Many of these traits can be seen together, as many empaths will experience one characteristic as a result of another. However, some traits do not develop right away. While empaths are quite intuitive and have basic instincts about using their emotions, a lot of empathic qualities develop due to circumstance. While researchers once believed that empathy is an innate ability that cannot be taught, it is now believed that empathic abilities can be developed and can change based on circumstances. In this regard, our environments and the people we surround ourselves with can affect how we recognize and express both our emotions and the emotions of others.

As mentioned earlier, empaths share many traits with highly sensitive people. Therefore, one characteristic of an empath is being highly sensitive. Do you ever get told that you are "too sensitive?" Do you find yourself being very personally affected by things that happen to other people and are told that you "care too much"? Then you may be an empath. Empaths internalize both their emotions and other people's, feeling them extremely deeply. If you consider yourself to be extremely sensitive to stimuli, then you are likely an empath. This can be to either emotional stimuli or even just noticing heightened senses.

Empaths are often prone to sensory overload, particularly in large crowds and social settings. Empaths are also known to dislike large crowds and small talk, due to the overwhelming feeling that big stimuli can cause. Because empaths take in so much and have a hard time controlling which stimuli their brains do and don't respond to, situations in which there is a lot going on, such as large gatherings or big crowds, can be very overwhelming and draining. Therefore, empaths are often shy and/or introverted, simply because being around people can be exhausting to them. It is common for empaths to need alone time in order to recharge. This can also go hand-in-hand with social anxiety, as empaths can become anxious around other people due to the intense activity going on in their brains.

Another common trait of an empath is taking on or internalizing other people's emotions. While most humans are able to experience empathy to a certain extent, empaths can completely absorb another person's feelings and feel the emotions as if they are their own. For instance, it is common for someone to understand and feel sad for a friend who just broke up with their significant other. However, an empath would take this sadness one step further and actually feel their friend's pain as if it were their own. If you often experience the pain of those close to you as if it were your own, then you are probably an empath.

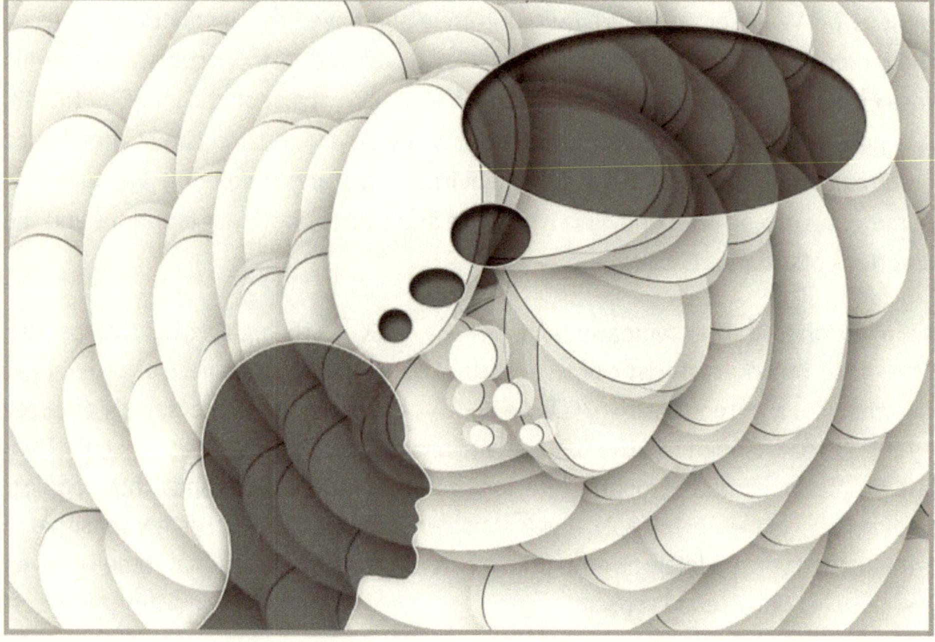

This can go for other emotions as well, but empaths can often even have trouble distinguishing where another person's feelings end and theirs start. For instance, have you ever spent time with someone who would not stop complaining about everything going wrong in their life, and then you came home in a bad mood? This is a characteristic of an empath, as they tend to internalize the emotions of others around them. This also means that they are able to pick up on and process the energies of other people, which can sometimes mean that they find themselves in a bad mood after spending time with negative people.

As mentioned earlier, empaths most commonly identify as introverts. An introvert is anyone who gets their energy from spending time alone, whereas extroverts get energy from spending time with other people. Empaths often become drained and need to recharge after social interactions and thus enjoy spending time alone. Empaths often run out of steam in large groups, and often prefer spending time with one person or a few people instead of spending time in large groups. Empaths also dislike big crowds of people, and often feel very overwhelmed, making them prone to social anxiety as well. This may seem like a contradiction, given that empaths are very people-oriented and are natural caretakers and helpers. However, they are introverts in the sense that they feel their energy being drained when they are around people too much. This is because they absorb other people's energy, but also put a lot of their own energy into others, which causes them to feel overwhelmed and drained.

Furthermore, another quality of being an empath is feeling like you are an outsider or do not fit in with other people. Even though empaths are highly sensitive and emotionally in tune with other people's feelings, this can end up resulting in feelings of loneliness. Those who identify as strong empaths can discover that other people do not feel as deeply as they do, causing them to not have very much in common. This can result in pushing others away and feelings of loneliness. Empaths can also have trouble maintaining close or intimate relationships. This might be because when they get close to someone, it can become difficult to distinguish the line between their personal emotions and the other person's emotions that they have internalized. Furthermore, especially if the other person is particularly negative, it can take a toll on the empath's personal feelings and vibrational field. This can cause the empath to internalize the negative energy.

Because of this, empaths can tend to avoid intimacy and/or becoming close to other people. They then often end up pushing other people away and/or isolating themselves, which can result in loneliness or the feeling of being an outsider. It is important that empaths first prioritize their relationships with themselves before putting all of their energy into other people. While this may seem like you are isolating yourself at first, it will actually be beneficial in the long run, as working on building a strong relationship with yourself is a good base for creating strong and healthy relationships with other people. You will find that by focusing on your internal energy, you will be much more in control of the external energy you are projecting and even internalizing, which will in turn have positive impacts on many different aspects of your life.

While these all seem like common side effects of being an empath, empaths also tend to have hyperactive senses, making them susceptible to sensory overload. If you find yourself overwhelmed by noises or smells, in addition to other qualities of being highly sensitive, you may identify as an empath. Furthermore, empaths often gravitate to nature. Similarly to recharging in solitude, nature can be energizing to empaths. Interestingly enough, empaths are also often drawn to the water. Water seems to energize them, and being near a large body of water can help an empath recharge. If you recognize any or multiple of these common signs in yourself, especially in conjunction with each other, you may identify as an empath. Let's now explore how the functions of an empath's brain can produce these tendencies and qualities.

Empathy And The Brain

Through evolution, humans have developed brains that are highly capable of picking up on the emotions of others, even subtle ones. We have become so capable of this, in fact, that some of us are able to not only sense the emotions and energies of others but internalize them as if they are our own. Many scientists believe that humans developed the ability to empathize in order to produce and care for their offspring. Researchers have also found evidence of this quality in other mammals who produce a smaller amount of offspring in comparison to non-mammals (*Lesley University, 2019*).

While we may be genetically predisposed to experiencing some sort of empathy, other factors including how we are raised and the environment in which we live can affect how this quality is further developed. Although some researchers believe that as children, the amount of empathy we display is the same amount we will have for the rest of our lives, others believe that empathy can easily be developed and improved upon. Another common speculation is that humans developed empathy for the purpose of mutualism, which helps the whole species survive and continue to reproduce (*Riess, 2017*).

Researchers have discovered that even unconsciously, humans tend to imitate the actions of each other. This can translate into emotions and feelings, as a person can see someone else expressing sadness and then feel it themselves. However, we generally feel the emotions of others to a lesser extent so as not to let it consume us.

For instance, if you were to find out that your friend is experiencing sadness over a bad breakup, you would probably also be sad for them, but you would not spend as much time grieving the end of their relationship as they would. This is because our brains are wired to respond to these stimuli in a manner that reduces the extent to which we feel the same emotions. Ultimately, this allows us to be more helpful to the person experiencing pain. For empaths, however, the response is different. Empaths are much more sensitive to these stimuli, causing them to feel the pain at a stronger degree than other people. This can result in them feeling the pain of others to a level almost equal to how the person experiencing the hardship feels it.

Many scientists believe that empathy involves different components. One component is a response to another person's emotions and/or behaviors, which is often feeling what they are feeling. The next component is the cognitive ability to adopt the other person's viewpoint when discussing an issue. Lastly, psychologists believe that empathy involves the action of regulating one's own thoughts on the matter (Decety & Moriguchi, 2007). When examining the different neurological processes that go into experiencing empathy, we can see how empaths' brains are essentially working overtime to absorb the emotions of people around them.

While most empathetic people experience all of these different components that go into empathy, empaths experience them to a heightened sense, hence the idea that they are working overtime. Their brains are essentially wired differently to not only regulate their own thoughts on the other person's emotions that they are experiencing but to actually internalize the emotions as their own. This is why it is so important that empaths begin to notice the energy and emotions that they are internalizing first before acting on them. This will change the way they are then able to regulate their own thoughts and emotions resulting from the energy they pick up from other people.

Another neurological aspect of empathy that differs between empaths and non-empaths is the concept of self-awareness. This is an important component of experiencing empathy because it avoids emotional contagion, or the inability to distinguish another person's feelings from one's own (*Decety & Moriguchi, 2007*). This is the area in which empaths struggle. Clearly empaths are very good at recognizing and acting on other people's emotions, but they are very susceptible to emotional contagion. Furthermore, much of the neurological processes that determine how we feel empathy are related to our perspective of ourselves, which is similar to self-awareness in that it is an understanding of our various standpoints. However, this is another concept that varies for empaths. While many researchers believe that we are more likely to empathize with those that we relate to or that share a common goal with us, empaths are able to empathize with anyone regardless of their relationship.

There are two extremes to the concept of empathy. As we've already established, someone who experiences as much empathy as possible is considered an empath. However, there are certain personality disorders in which humans display little to no empathy toward other people. People who possess very little empathy for others include narcissists and psychopaths. Looking at the biological functions behind empathy, the difference between an empath and a narcissist or psychopath is the way in which our mirror neurons work. Mirror neurons mediate the brain's response to observing emotions and reactions in other people.

Scientists have developed the theory that these neurons can actually simulate what someone is experiencing in our own minds so that we can directly empathize with them (*Lesley University, 2019*). According to this theory, when we empathize with someone, our brains are actually trying to simulate what they are going through so that we can essentially experience and/or feel the same thing. This relates again to the concept of self-awareness. In our brains, there is somewhat of an overlap between our self-focused processes and other-focused processes. This allows us to empathize with others by internalizing their emotions in order to understand them. Empaths likely have a higher overlap of self-focused and other-focused processes, often internalizing others' emotions as their own. Using the Simulation Theory, we can also begin to understand why empaths are so prone to getting overwhelmed or drained of their energy. When one is constantly simulating the feelings and emotions of another person in their own brain, burnout can seem inevitable.

Another aspect of empathy to consider is that many psychology researchers believe that there are two types of empathy that humans experience: emotional and cognitive. Emotional empathy describes the ways in which we can internalize the emotions of another person in order to feel compassion for them. (*Lesley University,* *2019*). This is at the root of altruism, which is commonly defined as being selfless in the pursuit of the well-being of other people. Emotional empathy is at play when we feel sad because our friends are sad. This is of course a common trait of empaths, as they are very sensitive to emotions and can feel them deeply, even if they did not originate as their own.

The second type of empathy, cognitive empathy, refers to how we are able to accurately understand and develop a correct perception of another person's emotions. Using the same example, this would manifest in how we would be able to identify that our friend is sad, why they are sad, and how they are sad instead of angry. Through cognitive processes, we identify the relationship between one's behavior and emotions (*Lesley University, 2019*). For instance, cognitive empathy would be at play when we recognize that our friend has been distancing themselves from us recently and not being present at social gatherings (their behavior) because they are sad about a recent break-up they went through (their emotions). Empaths are generally skilled in both emotional and cognitive empathy. They are generally very in tune with human behavior, so they are able to use observations to recognize human emotion, even if it has not been explicitly disclosed. They are also able to internalize another person's emotions and simulate what they are feeling, showing that they have high emotional empathy.

While many empaths can relate to internalizing others' emotions as their own, recent psychological research has found that between 1-2% of the population is made up of what is referred to as "super empaths." Super empaths can not only simulate the feelings of others but can literally experience their physical feelings. According to a 2018 research presentation at the ERSC's Festival of Social Sciences, this type of empathic trait is also referred to as mirror-touch synesthesia (*"Super Empaths" with Rare Condition Can Feel Your Pain - Economic and Social Research Council, 2018*). Synesthesia is defined as a condition in which two or more senses become difficult to distinguish. For instance, you may have met someone who says that certain sounds have a color to them. This is an example of synesthesia in that the senses of hearing and seeing blend together.

For super empaths, their synesthesia blends the senses of seeing and touching/feeling, in that if they can see another person being physically touched, then they can also feel it in their own body. The researchers also found that the people who experienced this "mirror-touch" phenomenon were also more likely to experience high levels of emotional empathy, picking up on very subtle energies and emotions (*"Super Empaths" with Rare Condition Can Feel Your Pain - Economic and Social Research Council, 2018*). This exhibits how empaths' neurological functions make them much more susceptible to picking up on and even internalizing the emotions of other people, so much so that they could even feel another person being touched.

Through understanding the way that empathy functions in the human brain, we are able to understand more about empaths themselves. Empaths experience the same empathic neurological functions as other people, but they are simply more sensitive and generally experience these processes to a higher degree. By distinguishing among the different neurological processes that inform our personalities and behaviors, we are able to better understand why we are the way we are, and how we can better develop our empathy in a way that best benefits us and those around us.

02

CHAPTER

Empaths - the Good & the Bad

- Benefits of Being an Empath

Now that we've established some of the characteristics of empaths, we can discuss how being an empath can impact a person's life. As already established, empaths have different levels of sensitivity to different stimulants, especially in social settings. However, this is not necessarily a bad thing. This just means that they tend to be more introverted and prefer spending time alone to recharge after social interactions. Just like any personality type, being an empath is not one-size-fits-all. There are many different qualities that apply to empaths, and many people experience different traits to different degrees.

Now let's discuss the ways in which identifying as an empath can be extremely beneficial, as well as the challenges that empaths can often face. Empaths also may experience some traits at certain times, while finding that different characteristics do not always apply to their specific circumstances. There are also different circumstances that can bring out different traits in a person. By recognizing your empathic characteristics, you can notice when you find yourself becoming distant or getting overwhelmed by stimulation. Big changes can also cause this to happen, so knowing your empathic qualities will help you stay grounded and prioritize self-care.

It is important to keep in mind that personality types and traits are extremely complex. One characteristic may seem like a gift one day and a curse the next. Furthermore, personalities are dynamic and can change and develop based on different factors like your environment, the people you surround yourself with, and your education. Therefore, many of the traits that empaths develop differ based on these factors, and these basic traits can end up functioning completely differently based on the person and their circumstances. For instance, whereas one person may love their hypersensitivity because it allows them to build deeper emotional connections with other people, another person may find that their hypersensitivity causes them to become overwhelmed and distance themselves from other people. This example illustrates how one common personality trait can have the opposite effect depending on the person. With this in mind, you can decide which traits you possess and how they manifest in your daily life in conjunction with your other characteristics. By looking at the parts and the whole of your personality, you will better be able to decide how you identify as an empath, and you will learn more about yourself and your personal skills, as well as the challenges you may face.

Benefits Of Being An Empath

Many of what we consider to be benefits of identifying as an empath lie within certain contradictions. Although an empath would probably consider themselves to be an introvert, many of their gifts also lie in being a people person. Because empaths are able to absorb the emotions and energy of other people around them, they are naturally very good at reading people. This also means that they generally have strong intuition and instincts, which can prove to be a very practical life skill. This is helpful in that they are good at picking out who is truthful and who is dishonest. While these skills can seem overwhelming at times, being a good judge of character is definitely a huge advantage for empaths. For non-empaths who have difficulty relating to other people, this intuition and character judgment may not come as easily, which can cause problems. Empaths are also able to tell when a person is lying to them, which can prove to be an essential skill in today's society. These gifts also help them excel in different professions that work with other people. Empaths often make great teachers, therapists, healthcare providers, business people, and any other role that requires a deep understanding of people. Being a strong predictor of human behavior is one of an empath's best assets.

Since they have strong judgment and intuition, empaths are also good at protecting themselves and others from threatening people. Have you ever met someone who you thought was just a little bit off? Maybe it was your friend's new significant other who had questionable motivations, and you turned out to be right. This is a common practical skill that empaths possess, and that likely goes back to the evolutionary roots of empathy. Empaths' ability to sense energy and emotions allows them to easily identify threats and protect themselves and others around them. This is another benefit of their gift of strong and accurate intuition. If you think that you have good intuition and your first instinct is generally right, but have not fully developed your skills, then you may still be an empath. Many empaths have intuition but it is dormant because they have not developed it. Furthermore, this strong intuition can be used for many different gifts, such as manifestation or lucid dreaming. In the next chapter, we will focus on how you can explore and develop your natural gifts.

Empaths are generally also very creative individuals. This is one of the gifts that come with an empathic personality that can be developed and honed, but empaths generally find that creativity comes naturally to them. Because empaths are so in touch with emotions and sensitive to different emotions, they are able to channel these feelings into creative expressions, such as art. While people who are closed off and separated from their emotions might have difficulty with creative blocks, empaths are generally naturally able to channel and express their emotions. Not only can they do this by tapping into their own emotions, but since they are so easily able to absorb the emotions of other people, they can express the emotions of others as well.

This creativity can translate into many different forms, such as art, writing, or even different spiritual practices. Channeling the emotions of others makes empaths understanding to the point of expression, which is a creative asset. Furthermore, this creativity can allow empaths to better explore the energy that flows within and without human beings. Through creative expression, empaths can better understand their own inner energy, which can help with both self-expression and the understanding of oneself. Through absorbing and channeling other peoples' emotions, empaths can actually become more in tune with their own thoughts and feelings.

Another gift that empaths possess is the ability to heal others. Since they can identify, understand, feel, and act on the emotions of others, this makes them very capable of deciding how to help people. This is one of the qualities that makes empaths such good therapists and doctors. However, empaths also make great holistic doctors and energy healers, as they are very in tune with the energy that other people project. Through healing other people, empaths can also feel as if they are healing themselves. If you identify as an empath, then you probably find yourself taking the role of mediator in many group settings.

When helping friends or family, do you find yourself feeling better as a result? This is because you are internalizing the negative energy when there is a problem. If your friends are fighting, even if you are not directly involved, you may feel upset and anxious as a result of all the negativity and sadness circulating around you. However, you can heal this energy that is negatively affecting both your friends and you by acting as a mediator. In a sense, this is actually helping you as you are improving the vibrations that surround you, allowing you to internalize more positive emotions. This is a large reason why empaths use their gift of healing, because by healing others, they can also heal themselves. This depicts the altruistic value of empathy. Empaths choose to help others because it makes them feel better. This is also why empaths are often able to feel extremely fulfilled in careers where they help others, such as in healthcare or counseling.

Empaths also have the special ability to create and nurture strong connections with other people. This can be extremely fulfilling, as they find that they have the ability to create extremely strong bonds with the people in their lives. Interestingly enough, empaths are also able to form these strong connections with animals in addition to humans. They are able to sense the emotions of different animals, and they also have a strong connection to nature. This compassionate ability to create bonds with different people and even animals is a gift to empaths, as it provides fulfillment. Empaths, though introverted, ultimately crave connection. Because they are so skilled at absorbing energy and emotions, they are easily able to build these connections, which leads to emotional fulfillment. This makes empaths good partners, friends, and family members.

Ultimately, having these strong emotional abilities and the capability to create deep emotional bonds allows empaths to attract a lot of love and positivity into their lives. Furthermore, while feeling other people's pain and sadness can seem like a disadvantage of being an empath, they also feel other people's happiness and love. Essentially, when empaths feel joy, they feel it at a heightened sense, which is one of their greatest gifts. These are all gifts that allow empaths to create strong and special emotional connections with other people. These connections also allow them to excel in different aspects of their lives, especially in interpersonal situations. Empaths are generally very well-liked, making them good friends, partners, co-workers, etc. This allows them to feel comfortable and appreciated in social situations, which can in turn put them more at ease in the case of overstimulation. This is one of the greatest gifts that comes with being an empath, and these strong bonds often provide support through some of the setbacks that empaths may face.

Setbacks Of Being An Empath And How To Overcome Them

While being an empath certainly is a gift that many people appreciate having, it does come with its fair share of challenges. If you identify as an empath, then many of these challenges may apply to you even if you have not officially labeled or even noticed them. Whether you find that you are susceptible to all of the traits described or not, identifying them is key to knowing how to deal with some of the external challenges that arise with being an empath. Furthermore, you may see an overlap among some of these common challenges and a lot of the gifts you possess that we just went over. This is because many of the qualities that empaths possess can be good or bad, all depending on the context. You may not have given this much thought in the past. But by identifying these qualities now, you can identify how they are both negatively and positively affecting your life, and how you can become more in tune with yourself. As an empath, you are likely very in tune with the emotions and energy of other people. But by teaching you about what makes you you, this book can help you become more in tune with yourself.

As already mentioned as a characteristic of empaths, overstimulation is a common challenge that empaths face. Since their brains are essentially hypersensitive to different stimuli, empaths can easily become overwhelmed and drained in settings where they are surrounded by a lot of people and/or activity. Empaths especially can encounter this in situations even with people they are close to, simply because they require time alone to recharge. You may have encountered this in a school or workplace setting. Has a friend ever asked you to grab dinner after work, but you simply could not imagine spending even more time with other people after 8 hours of constant stimulation? This is nothing to be ashamed of — it just means that you recharge by spending time alone.

If you find yourself in a profession or living situation that requires you to frequently be surrounded by other people, there are some precautions you can take to avoid the effects of overstimulation. Self-care, specifically for empaths (which we will discuss in later chapters) is extremely important to make sure that we are allowing ourselves to recover from overstimulation and burnout. Another thing that empaths can do to incorporate some alone time to recharge is taking breaks or maintaining some sort of distance. If you live with roommates and feel like you are too constantly surrounded by people, it is perfectly valid to lock yourself in your room for some alone time. People are generally very understanding, as no one wants to spend time with someone who is clearly drained and not themself.

Another challenge that empaths commonly face in their daily lives is an overload of negative energy. This can be in any situation, but if you find yourself surrounded by negative people who cannot stop complaining, or you find yourself also getting upset after checking the news, this is probably a sign that you need some self-care. In later chapters, we will also focus on energy healing for empaths. Since empaths are so easily able to pick up on even the most subtle energy around them, if they are around many negative people, they might find themselves drained or emotionally distraught as a result. To avoid this overwhelming sensation, it is very important to practice self-care, energy healing, and solitary activities.

You may also find that you need to spend less time with the people that are draining you of your energy or causing you to feel negative emotions whenever you are around them. This is also a form of self-care — cutting consistently negative people out of your life is important, especially for empaths, in order to protect and ensure your own happiness. Of course, this is easier said than done, and another challenge empaths face is that they tend to attract these negative people. If you feel as if you are always attracting negative energy into your life and have no idea how to stop, especially in social situations, this is the book for you. Identifying that you may be susceptible to these traits is the first step. Once you start noticing who and what is causing you to constantly feel negative emotions or be emotionally drained, you can start to figure out where you can heal.

Another side effect that empaths face is a trait that was mentioned earlier: loneliness. This is another contradiction that empaths provide us with, as one would assume that an empath would be a people person. However, loneliness can be common among empaths, especially those who isolate themselves from other people when they become overwhelmed and drained. A common setback of being an empath is being overwhelmed to the point of distance. There is a fine line between taking necessary alone time to recharge and distancing yourself too much so that you become lonely, and when stimulation is high empaths can often find themselves struggling with this. Empaths can also find that they push people away in close relationships due to the struggle of constant overstimulation. This can lead to loneliness and a feeling that other people do not understand them.

Another trait of empaths that can lead to isolation is their insight into other people's characters. This can cause them to come off as judgemental or standoffish, which can be off-putting to others. However, this is ultimately a good quality, as it allows you to ensure that the people in your life are good for you. It also allows you to build friendships and relationships on genuine connections rather than just surface-level commonalities, which is ultimately beneficial. However, if you want to work on this simply to make a better first impression, there are steps you can take to avoid distancing yourself from others.

Another possible negative side effect of being an empath could be the increased susceptibility of mental illness. Empaths are often diagnosed, or misdiagnosed, with social anxiety, because of their tendency to become overwhelmed and anxious in settings with many people. Empaths are also more likely than average to develop other mental illnesses such as depression or substance use disorders as a result of attempting to cope with overstimulation (*The Hazards of Being an Empath*, 2020). According to Dr. Orloff's research, empaths can be at risk of developing substance use disorders as a way to try and escape the overstimulation they may face. Because empaths are essentially "sponges" to other people's feelings, being surrounded by too much negative energy can make them more likely to develop a substance addiction. Drugs and alcohol often numb or distract from the heightened sensations that an empath's hypersensitive brain experiences, causing them to rely on these substances.

Empaths are also prone to anxiety, depression, and other disorders simply because their brains are hypersensitive. While a non-empath may be able to brush off certain negative events, empaths don't have the same capability to do so. This can result in the development of different disorders (*The Hazards of Being an Empath*, 2020). However, with proper care and treatment, empaths are able to develop and practice safe coping mechanisms. This is why it is extremely important to stay self-aware and keep in touch with your inner self. Noticing your behavior patterns and knowing when to get help will be very beneficial in the long run, as you will be able to recognize whether you have an addictive personality and/or a susceptibility to any mental illnesses.

There are many other challenges empaths face in regard to their sensitivity and compassion. While these are good things, empaths can often feel as if other people are taking advantage of them. Empaths are naturally caring and compassionate people, which can cause them to attract people that take advantage of their kindness and essentially drain their energy. Empaths are also often told they are "too sensitive," which can result in strained relationships. This can also create difficulties, especially in early life, with forming relationships with other people. Empaths can sometimes face difficulties in school situations, as they are still learning how to cope with their empathic traits while also learning how to form new relationships with other people. It is not uncommon for empaths to face difficulties making friends, especially in large groups, because of how hypersensitive they are.

They are also prone to having difficulties with boundary setting. Since empaths are so compassionate and want to help others with their emotions, this can be another way in which they are taken advantage of. People can cross boundaries, expecting too much from empaths. As a result, empaths often find themselves unable to say "no," emotionally exhausted, and feeling taken-for-granted. They can also feel as if they attract people that take advantage of them in this regard, which can lead to them consistently entering toxic relationships. This is also because empaths ultimately often crave the feeling of helping other people and want to feel as if they are taking care of others. However, this can lead to toxic relationships and bad patterns.

This is why learning to set boundaries is a form of self-care. Through setting boundaries, empaths can ensure that they no longer feel as if the people around them are taking them for granted. It will also prevent emotional burnout. Lastly, empaths can struggle with self-care. Even though this is extremely important in order to recharge, empaths often put others' needs before their own. This can be detrimental behavior, as neglecting your own feelings can end up negatively affecting your relationships with others. By prioritizing your own mental and emotional well-being, you will find that you can be a better version of your empathic self.

03

CHAPTER

Empaths & Spirituality

➤ What Is Spirituality?

As we've previously mentioned, empaths have many skills related to different spiritual practices. Empaths are typically very in tune with energy and intuition, making them likely to possess clairvoyant or psychic abilities. However, even if you do not think you are psychic, your empathic abilities may make you more likely to believe in different spiritual processes such as energy healing, manifestation, chakra balancing, and meditation. While there are a great number of different spiritual processes that empaths might find themselves gravitating towards, we are going to focus more broadly on spirituality in general.

Western culture does not necessarily provide us with a great number of tools to develop our intuitive gifts into a lifestyle. Therefore, many of us are probably not even aware of these gifts that we possess. A lot of spirituality that concerns energy patterns and a person's intuition can often be written off as "mumbo jumbo." However, an empath's intuition is one of their greatest gifts, and learning how to tap into it is a great way to become more in tune with your emotions and energy flows. This will then help you better connect with others, and you will see the benefits of learning how to better control your own energy flows.

If you have ever felt as if you experience some weird coincidences or deja vu often, this might be an example of your inner intuition at work unconsciously. You may not realize it, but your intuition could still be strong inside of you, but it has just been suppressed. Even if you do not feel as if you have strong natural intuition, however, you can still develop these skills and work to improve it. Before we discuss how we can work on developing our skills, let's first delve into what spirituality is and how this applies to empaths.

What Is Spirituality?

There is no one basic definition of spirituality, mainly because it encompasses such a large part of the human experience and can be applied to many different aspects of life. Generally, spirituality can be defined as the connection between a human being and what they believe to be a larger being or process (*What Is Spirituality?* | *Taking Charge of Your Health & Wellbeing*, 2019). Spirituality is often defined as the search for purpose or meaning. This search can take place within or without the human body and spirit. However, spirituality is a common and age-old aspect of human existence. It mainly refers to our feelings of connectedness and purpose, and we can often discover more about our personal beliefs by looking inwards.

Some people feel this connection in religion and participate in worship in order to feel that connection to a larger being. Some people believe in the concept of the universe being an overarching being, and they choose to participate in different practices that connect them to the universe, such as manifestation or meditation. Some people believe that we can connect to this larger being by tuning in to our own energy. This is where intuition comes into play, and we will focus mainly on this aspect of our spirituality in order to control and monitor our own energy flows and processes. It is important to note that how we express our spirituality is not clear-cut. One can believe in a higher power in a religious sense, while also believing that they are an empath with a strong intuition and the ability to pick up on other people's energies.

However you choose to express your spirituality, you can learn something based on your own specific energy and processes. Spirituality, while sometimes a collective experience, is really all about creating your personal connection to whatever higher power you believe in. This means focusing your energy inward in order to tap into your energetic source and create that connection with whatever higher power you are trying to connect with. You can find out a lot about yourself, your energy, and the world around you through connecting with your natural intuition. As an empath, this natural intuition is likely strong already, which will allow you to really tap into your energy source and create those energetic flows between yourself and the higher power.

Psychological researcher Howard Clinebell developed 7 criteria that humans often apply their search for meaning to. These criteria are what they often look for in their practice of spirituality (*What Is Spirituality?* | *Taking Charge of Your Health & Wellbeing*, 2019). Clinebell determined that the 7 criteria, which he outlined in a 1992 book, are mind, body, spirit, love, play, and the world. To relate this to spirituality, each of these concepts is something that we search for in ourselves and in our attempt to find meaning. For instance, we search for love, whether it be in ourselves or with others. This is something that empaths often hold as a main priority, as ultimately they want to experience the love that they are able to feel so sensitively and give so freely. However, where empaths can go wrong in their spiritual journey is in their outward search for love instead of looking inward. Through getting more in tune with their own emotions, empaths can find a good balance, so as to find fulfillment inwards and not feel like they have to search for it in anyone else.

Human beings also inherently search for something bigger than themselves, striving to create a connection. This is something that empaths often do without even realizing it. By tuning in to and understanding other people's energies, they are able to feel a connection beyond just themselves. These are just a few examples of how empaths often build a spiritual connection without even realizing it. These criteria are essentially the ways in which we often look for fulfillment through spirituality. For instance, we can look for fulfillment through physical movement; many exercises, such as yoga, serve as spiritual actions, as connecting our body to a higher power allows us to feel in control and allows us to raise our energetic vibrations. We also look for fulfillment on an intellectual level as it relates to the mind. We seek to increase our knowledge and our capacity to increase our intellectual abilities. Through these different criteria, we find ourselves in pursuit of an energetic and spiritual connection as we seek fulfillment in our lives.

Empaths may also find that spiritual healing is what they need to move past their need for fulfillment and connection. Dr. Orloff, who is not only an empath but has done extensive research on empaths, developed the term "energy psychiatry" as a way to blend spirituality with the traditional practice of psychiatric care in order to heal the mind, body, and spirit. This method was developed to use subtle energetics as a way of healing (Mason, 2005). This allows us to tap into our energetic power, which Orloff believes is often made to lie dormant. This concept exhibits how we can use different forms of spirituality in order to build a greater connection with our spirit and the world and energy around us.

Orloff specifically mentions the benefits of practices such as meditation and Reiki energy healing, which are often considered to be forms of alternative medicine. Furthermore, Orloff cites the importance of the concept of intuition in healing, stating that intuition can increase inner guidance. As empaths naturally have a strong intuition, through using different spiritual practices to strengthen this gift, they can find that they are able to look inwards in healing (Mason, 2005). Furthermore, in developing one's own intuition, doctors and healers can actually be more helpful to patients. This again ties into the ways in which empaths are inherently good healers and can help others. By creating a strong connection with one's own mind and body, a person can pick up on all the subtle energies that flow within and without the body. Essentially, through strengthening the inner process of intuition, we can find that many of the answers to the questions we seek lie within us.

For instance, this ties into processes such as manifestation and meditation. Both of these spiritual processes require us to look inwards in order to create our spiritual connections. Empaths are often very skilled at using their intuition to harness energy, simply because they are able to pick up on subtle energy flows. This makes it very easy for empaths to use their spiritual gifts, sometimes without even consciously thinking about it. Empaths are naturally skilled at picking up on energetic vibrations. When they apply this to actions like manifestation and actually channel the energy that they are able to pick up on, they are generally very successful in knowing what they need and how to attract this. In the next sections, we will discuss how empaths can work to develop their skills of intuition and apply them to spiritual processes.

But first, let's start by defining some terms and describing some processes. Your intuition refers to your inherent ability to understand something solely based on unconscious instinct, not on logic or reasoning. As an empath, you definitely have a strong intuition, whether you often consciously notice it or not. Have you ever encountered a moment where you were told to do one thing, but you had a gut feeling telling you to do another? This is your intuition at work. This further exhibits how empathy can be a survival skill. By having these strong intuitive skills, humans are able to protect themselves and their lives. It also allows you to be a strong judge of character, which is a very valuable life skill.

One way in which many people get in touch with their intuition is through dreaming. Empaths, as very creative and intuitive individuals, are known to have very vivid dreams. These dreams can provide them with insight and clarity into their own perceptions of the world. A common phenomenon that empaths may experience is the sense that things that happen in their dreams come true in real life. This is your intuition at work in your mind, even when you are unconscious. Now, this is not necessarily referring to being able to predict huge events like a tornado or a stock market crash (although some people claim to be able to do this), but rather smaller predictable events that occur in everyday life. Have you ever just randomly gotten a sense of deja vu when doing something completely random, like sitting in class or driving to work? This is your intuition at work. Though this can seem as if it is just a random sensation, there are actually ways to tap into your intuition as it manifests in your dreams.

We will get into techniques in the next sections, but another way of seeing your intuition play out in your dreams is through lucid dreaming. Lucid dreaming is a phenomenon that, although studied by researchers, is not fully understood by humans. Essentially, a lucid dream is when you are asleep and dreaming, but you are consciously aware that what is happening in your dream is not real. This basically puts you in control of your dream, allowing you to be the director of the movie rather than just a cast member. Lucid dreaming occurs when you are having a very vivid dream, but you are aware that the events occurring in your dream are not real, which in a sense separates your conscious mind from your unconscious mind.

Have you ever had a nightmare and then found yourself thinking 'this isn't real,' while still having the dream? This is an example of lucid dreaming. Lucid dreaming can provide us with a sense of control that we can carry into our everyday lives. By learning to lucid dream, we can also tap into our intuition by controlling how it is expressed. Lucid dreaming can even be used as a type of therapy for people who have chronic nightmares. Even if you do not find yourself often having these sorts of dreams, but you want to see if you can start to control your unconscious intuition, there are techniques that allow you to develop your ability to lucid dream.

Another way that you can get in touch with your intuition is through the practice of meditation. Meditation is an age-old practice that involves sitting with and observing your thoughts, allowing them to flow freely while also often focusing on your breath as you do so. However, this definition is extremely broad, and there are countless ways and forms of meditation. Essentially, meditation is a way to connect with your inner energy and intuition by allowing your brain to observe and get in touch with the unconscious. Meditation is often used as a spiritual practice, either in conjunction with other practices or by itself, and can even be used in therapy and holistic medical treatments. There are many proven benefits of meditation, and empaths specifically can meditate in order to re-balance their energy and recharge after long periods of social interaction.

There are also different forms of meditation, but the main ones include focused meditation and free meditation. In focused meditation, you focus on something, whether that be on the flow of your breath or a guided meditation. This allows you to fixate your mind on something so that you can keep it from wandering. Free forms of meditation, however, allow you to just let your thoughts flow in and out. You do not necessarily focus on anything, but you simply notice your thoughts and then release them. This is a great way for empaths to start grounding themselves. By meditating and noticing your thoughts, then releasing them without reacting to them, you will find that you can exercise control of what you let affect you and what you respond to. This will then allow you to exercise this control in your everyday life, and you will find it much easier to stop other people's energies from affecting you so deeply.

Another spiritual process that is often related to dreaming, intuition, and meditation is the concept of manifestation. Manifestation is a technique that uses the laws of energy and the universe and essentially focuses on the idea that the energy that we project is the energy that will come to us. This technique has recently become very popular in the realms of self-help and spirituality and is often used in conjunction with meditation. There are even certain methods and techniques that suggest that you can manifest in your dreams. Whatever the case, manifestation is often extremely successful when done by a particularly intuitive person, simply because it requires intense focus and in order to work, it needs you to be very clear and specific about the emotions that will result from whatever it is you are manifesting.

In the next section, we will get into manifestation techniques that prove to be particularly useful for empaths. This technique uses the Law of Attraction in order to work. The Law of Attraction is an energetic law that states that the energy we put out is what we attract. For instance, if you truly believe that you are going to have a good day, and keep repeating that to yourself throughout the day, you will find yourself focusing on the positive things that happen to you, and you will most likely have a good day. However, if you keep thinking and speaking negatively, convincing yourself that you are going to have a bad day, you are probably going to have a bad day. This is because the energy we are putting out into the universe is what we are attracting back into our lives. Furthermore, when we are focusing on a certain thought or idea, this is what we will notice in our lives. This may still sound a little confusing, so we will get into this practice in the next section.

Developing Your Intuition

If some of these processes sound intriguing to you but you still do not completely understand how to make spirituality work in your everyday life, then look no further than this book. There are many ways that you can tap into the feelings of both yourself and others in order to develop your intuition and apply it to different spiritual and healing processes. One common process that empaths are particularly skilled in is energy healing, which we will discuss in detail in the next chapter. However, despite natural gifts that make empaths skilled at different processes that express their intuition, there are many things that take practice and technique to develop. Remember that spirituality is a journey — it may seem kind of difficult to practice harnessing your intuition and energy at first, but as you keep going you will figure out what is best for you. You will also become more in tune to your own emotions and energy, which will show you how to be more in balance with both yourself and the higher power you believe in. Finding inner harmony is the best way to harness your energy into a spiritual journey and find fulfillment. Once you tap into this energy source, you will find yourself focusing on gratitude and the positive aspects of your life, in turn protecting this energy.

For instance, you have just read about what lucid dreaming is, and you may now be wondering to yourself about how people actually do this frequently, and how they are able to use it to improve their lives. If you want to learn how to lucid dream but aren't sure where to start, here are some tips. One way to start lucid dreaming is to practice testing your reality. As an empath, you often find yourself becoming overstimulated by your brain, which can cause you to get wrapped up in your thoughts. If you find this happening throughout the day, you can start by grounding yourself. Attempt to "test" your reality, by asking yourself if what is happening around you is actually real life. By doing this when you are conscious and feel yourself getting wrapped up in your thoughts, your brain will remember how to go through these motions when unconscious. Then you will hopefully be able to do this in your sleep, reminding yourself to check your reality even when you're unconscious and dreaming.

Another strategy that can help you lucid dream is waking up in the middle of the night and then going back to sleep. People often do this if they wake up randomly in the middle of the night, so if you set an alarm in order to purposely wake up, consciously remind yourself of your surroundings and the fact that you are awake, and then go back to sleep, you should find it easier to feel in control of your dreams.

Another strategy that helps with lucid dreaming, and with monitoring your dreams in general, is keeping a dream journal in which you record your dreams when you first wake up. Many people forget their dreams throughout the day, so recording them as soon as you wake up while they're still fresh in your head is a good way to remember the emotions that occurred in your dreams. This is also a good way to keep track of any patterns or predictions that arise in your dreams, and it can be a good way for empaths to notice their emotions and their unconscious expression of them. Keeping in touch with the unconscious self is a great way for empaths to feel a connection to their inner energy source.

Another spiritual practice that requires some technique and repetition is meditation. As we've established earlier, there are many different forms of meditation. You may choose to do a guided meditation or to just sit and observe your breath patterns. You may meditate with the intent of manifesting, or you may want to heal your energy and balance your chakras. Whatever the case, many people often struggle with being still and observing their own emotions and thoughts. For empaths in particular, this may present a challenge, simply because empaths often have active minds and are flooded with emotions and stimuli. However, once you are able to move past these distractions, you will find that meditating is a great way to ground yourself and recharge if you are feeling overwhelmed or drained.

It is important to keep in mind that there are different techniques for meditating, and there is not one that is better than the other. Rather, it is important to find what works best for you. For instance, you could choose to meditate while focusing your mind on one specific thing, such as your breath. For many empaths, this is a good route as it gives you more of a sense of control. It can keep your mind from wandering too much, allowing you to truly relax. It also helps to ground you, as focusing on your breath allows you to come back to the practice of meditation if you feel yourself distracted by your thoughts. However, you do not have to focus on the process of inhaling and exhaling as you meditate. You could choose to simply observe the thoughts that cross your mind, and then just let them go. This could also be a great technique for empaths, as it allows you to observe the energy and emotions that are taking up a lot of the space in your mind.

However, this technique can be difficult if you often get overstimulated and find your mind wandering. This is because it requires you to simply notice a thought, whether it be about your surroundings or something going on in your life, and then just let it go without reacting or thinking about it. Since empaths are prone to overthinking, it takes practice to release your thoughts in this way. This is why focusing on your breath is often a good way to start meditating. This can ultimately stabilize your emotions and help you become more in touch with your emotions. You can also try guided meditations, which are generally produced in the form of videos in which a narrator talks and reminds you what to focus on. This can be another great way to start off meditating and can be great if you are meditating with a certain goal in mind. This can also be a good tool for manifesting.

Another great way to channel your natural intuition is through manifestation. This is often done with meditation, as meditating before and after you manifest increases clarity and allows you to tap into your inner energy source to truly get what you need. While manifestation is obviously a very complicated process, and there is not necessarily a "right" way to do it, we will outline a brief guide on how you can start manifesting in your own life. The first step in manifestation is, of course, to clearly decide what it is you want to manifest and attract. Empaths are lucky in that their natural intuition allows them to clearly see what it is they need and want to attract into their lives.

It is important to focus on the feelings associated with what you are manifesting — you may even just be manifesting a feeling itself, like more happiness or love into your life. It is then important to visualize what you are trying to manifest. Empaths are also skilled at doing this because their intuition allows them to be very creative and very good at visualization. Visualization is an important step in manifestation, as it is important to create the feelings that you will have when you have manifested what you want. Essentially, you have to believe that you already have what it is that you are trying to attract. This is a technique that you can do through meditation, or even lucid dreaming, in order to make your visualization more effective.

After you've visualized, it is important to release the thought. Do not focus on what you want but do not have, because focusing on this lack will simply attract more lack. Rather, live your life with the feeling that you have what you want. You can also take action to achieve what you want while also carrying this feeling. For instance, if you want to attract more love into your life, express gratitude for all the love that you currently have. Then, love yourself and apply all of this love to your own spirit and to the strong relationships you have. By expressing gratitude for all the good things you currently have in your life, you will be able to attract more of them.

04

CHAPTER

Empaths & Energy

➤ How Do Empaths Affect Energy Flows?

In the past few chapters, we've briefly mentioned the concept of energy healing, and how empaths are generally very in tune with the energy of both themselves and others, but now we are really going to delve into the concept of energy. Energy is a driving force of life, and can be used to represent all sorts of things. Biologically, energy is what keeps us alive and moving. However, in order to understand the way that empaths work on a spiritual level, we will look at the term "energy" in its spiritual sense.

Like many of the other concepts we've defined thus far, energy can refer to and be applied to a lot of different processes and concepts. However, the term "energy" typically refers to someone's inner source. People can often also refer to energy as one's essence, aura, or "vibe." A person's "energy" is also connected to and refers to their inner force. If you've ever heard somebody say that they don't like a person's energy, this can mean that they feel as if it does not align with their own. We can also often internalize negativity around us, letting it cloud our energy. This, in turn, can make us more negative.

Empaths are particularly susceptible to these behaviors since they internalize so much of the energy around them. Energy is constantly flowing all around us, and for empaths, this is often extremely noticeable. While we may not always be consciously thinking about the energy that is surrounding us, empaths can find that this has a subconscious impact on what they are doing. For instance, if you have ever been in a library during finals week, you have probably found yourself feeling even more anxious after leaving than when you entered the library. This is because you were internalizing all of the anxious energy around you. This often applies to empaths, which is why it can be so hard for them to spend a lot of time in social situations, especially crowds.

Energy healing is an age-old process, and explaining the way energy works in a spiritual sense could be its own book. For the purposes of clarity, we can start by explaining different belief systems that focus on energy healing. One concept of energy that is applied to many different practices, such as yoga, energy healing, acupuncture, and meditation, is the idea of chakras. The term "chakra" is a Sanskrit word that refers to the source of one's energy. Chakras are key to different practices in many Hindu and Buddhist beliefs. There are 7 chakras, and each one is an energy source in the body that focuses on different parts of a person's life. It is believed that a person's energy flows within and without their chakras, and that energy can become blocked in one or multiple chakras, which can cause negative effects in one's life. In order to fix this, it is necessary to maintain aligned chakras and clear any energy blockages. This can often be achieved through yoga, meditation, or different specific practices depending on the chakra. Later in this chapter, we will explore common places to remedy blockage that are specific for empaths. However, we will first outline each of the chakras.

01 Root Chakra

The first chakra is referred to as the root chakra, and it can be found at the base of the spine. It is associated with the color red and with the functions of grounding, support, foundation, and security. Signs of an imbalance of the root chakra can be a feeling that you lack stability, a sense of isolation, or insecurity. This can be a common problem that empaths face, as they can become overwhelmed easily due to change and overstimulation. When this happens, it is important to ground yourself. The root chakra can be unblocked by engaging in grounding activities, like self-reflection, spending time in nature, and staying in a comfortable environment. We can also heal the root chakra through meditation and yoga.

02 Sacral Chakra

The second chakra is the sacral chakra, which is located in the pelvic region. It is associated with the color orange and the functions of pleasure, intimacy, and creativity. Many empaths can find that it is easy for them to align their sacral chakras, as they are naturally intuitive and creative. Signs of an imbalance in the sacral chakra can be problems with intimacy and expressing emotions and difficulty expressing passion. The sacral chakra can be unblocked by engaging in creative activities, dealing with pent-up emotions, yoga, and mediation. This also often occurs when empaths have trouble in relationships or are unable to express their emotions. Recharging and spending alone time to notice your emotions is a great way to unblock this chakra.

03 Solar Plexus Chakra

The third chakra is the solar plexus chakra, also referred to as the Manipura. It is located in the stomach. It is associated with the color yellow and relates to many inner functions like self-esteem, confidence, and motivation. This can be a common source of energy blockage for empaths, as a lot of their energy is derived from that of other people. Signs that this chakra is imbalanced include a lack of self-confidence and drive. The Manipura can be unblocked through yoga, meditation to tap into your inner purpose, and goal planning. If you find yourself struggling with your Manipura, make sure to tap into your own inner source and explore your own emotions, rather than focusing on other people's.

04 Heart Chakra

The fourth chakra is the heart chakra, located around the heart and lungs. Associated with the color green, this chakra is connected with love and compassion, both inner and outer. Signs that this chakra is blocked include a lack of self-love, issues in relationships with other people, and refusing love. The heart chakra is an extremely common source of energy blockage for empaths. A lack of self-love can result from closing yourself off or internalizing too much negative energy, which can in turn affect relationships. However, as an empath, you may also find that your heart chakra is somewhat overactive. As someone who is deeply connected to other people, you may find yourself putting too much energy into others, but neglecting your own self. This can result in insecurity and low self-esteem, which is why it is incredibly important to learn how to put yourself first. This chakra can be unblocked through meditation, yoga, and practicing self-love through affirmations.

05 Throat Chakra

The fifth chakra is the throat chakra, which is associated with the color blue. Its functions include communication, expression, and the voice. Empaths obviously care deeply about other people's feelings, sometimes putting them above their own. They are also prone to attracting people that suck up their energy. As a result, they can feel as if they are constantly being talked over or that their needs and feelings are being put beneath other people's. A blocked throat chakra is characterized by an inability to express thoughts and feelings and problems with communication. This chakra can be unblocked through meditation, affirmations, breathwork, and journaling.

06 Third-Eye Chakra

The sixth chakra is the third-eye chakra, located in between the eyes. It is associated with the color purple and the functions of intuition and inner reflection. Empaths naturally have a very open and active third-eye chakra, due to their strong intuition. However, even empaths can experience blockages here, especially if they have suppressed their natural intuitive gifts or allowed them to become dormant. A blocked third-eye chakra is characterized by a feeling of disconnect with your inner self and a lack of clear intuition. Even if you do have strong empathic intuition, you may find yourself feeling disconnected from your own feelings because you are so focused on the emotions of others. This chakra can be unblocked through time alone, self-reflection, and meditation.

07 Crown Chakra

The last chakra is the crown chakra, located right at the top of the head. This chakra is associated with the color white, and it focuses on the energy flow in our outer surroundings. It functions to connect our inner energy flows with the outside universe. By tapping into our inner energy source, we are able to connect with the universe around us. Empaths are naturally gifted in this regard, as they are very in tune with the energy flowing around them. A blocked crown chakra can manifest in the form of being close-minded or a feeling of disconnect in the universe around you. This chakra can be unblocked through meditation, yoga, and affirmations to reconnect with the outside world.

Understanding the way energy flows in different regions of the body dictated by different chakras allows us to focus on bringing different aspects of our lives into balance. Through understanding the way energy can become blocked or even overactive in the chakras, we can even gain insight about physical ailments that occur in different parts of the body. After explaining some of the ways in which our energy flows, we can now delve into how this specifically relates to empaths.

How Do Empaths Affect Energy Flows?

Since empaths are so easily able to literally feel another person's emotions, they often pick up on other people's energy flows. However, this can mean that if they are not paying attention, they can confuse another person's energy for their own. For instance, by spending a lot of time with a particularly anxious person, an empath can find themselves feeling stressed out. It can then be hard to distinguish if this feeling of anxiety is their own, or if it is instead the anxious energy they are picking up on from another person.

In this way, empaths can seem to enhance whatever energy it is they're picking up on, whether good or bad. They can act as a sort of catalyst for the energy that is being projected around them — internalizing it and then projecting out more of the same energy in return. However, this can be a good thing if empaths are able to ground themselves and learn how to harness positive energy. When they are able to project the positive energy they have internalized, they can in turn raise the vibrations around them. This is why people are often so attracted to empaths; they put them in a good mood when they are around them, and this makes for strong relationships.

Empaths also tend to pick up on all of the energy surrounding them, even if it is typically undesirable. They think of energy as a collective being and something that is shared among different spirits. Whereas some non-empaths are good at protecting their energy and are typically unfazed by what is going on with other people, empaths are much too sensitive to do this. Rather, they are seemingly unable to block out the stimulators around them, many of those stimulators being the energy patterns they are picking up on. They then become likely to internalize this energy. It is important to remember that energy blockages can also get pent up inside our bodies, causing imbalances in different aspects of our lives. Especially for empaths, setting boundaries is key. Not only will this allow you to protect your emotions and recharge, but boundary-setting also allows you to protect your energy from internalizing any negative vibrations. Having pent up or blocked energy can even affect our physical health. Different chakras govern different areas of the body, and different physical ailments are associated with the chakras.

Another energy concept, similar to chakras, is the idea of energy meridians. Meridians are often applied to Chinese medicine, and it is thought that there is a sort of connected pathway of different energy sources that flow throughout the body. These meridians are focused in each organ and form sort of a map for our energy to flow through our bodies (*Meridian Connection | TCM World*, 2019). The meridians not only fulfill biological functions and maintain homeostasis in our bodies, but they also provide a free flow of energy. This allows our 'chi' or 'qi,' which is believed to be our main energy force that flows throughout us, to flow through the body.

Maintaining a strong balance of chi is an important priority, and this is why humans participate in practices like yoga or meditation. Like an empath's brain, their meridian network is also extremely sensitive. Think of an empath's energy network, whether it be their chakras or their meridians, as similar to how their brain works. The empath's brain is hypersensitive to stimulators; their energy flow is no different. Empaths' energy flows are not only sensitive to whatever is happening to them personally but to other people's energy as well. Because of this, empaths may often find their energy to be unbalanced and need healing. This is why it is so important for empaths to recharge and spend time alone so as to somewhat cleanse their energy. However, it is also very important for empaths to know different healing techniques, which we will go over in the next section, that they can apply to their energy networks.

Energy Healing For Empaths

Dr. Orloff, having developed the idea of energy psychiatry, believes that energy healing is a very effective addition to other healthcare methods, and particularly so for empaths. Orloff believes that developing intuition is key to both healing oneself and healing others, and that doing so is a process that can be learned and practiced. Therefore, anyone can work on and build their intuition, regardless of whether or not it comes naturally to them (Mason, 2005). By developing a strong intuition, you are taking the first step to healing, simply by being able to become more in tune with your energy and emotions to see how exactly you need to heal.

Even if you believe that you are naturally hypersensitive to subtle energy, either in yourself or in others, this skill may be pushed down or dormant in you because you are not encouraged to use it. Increasing your intuition can in itself be a step towards healing, as you are able to become more in tune with your energy and emotions. Doing so also allows you to learn how to create barriers to block negative energy from affecting you as deeply as it currently may.

This is also a form of healing in that it allows you to have a greater sense of control. A common struggle for empaths is feeling a lack of control, especially over their emotions and the way that they react to the expression of energy and emotions around them. Becoming more in tune with your own emotions, through meditation, energy healing and manifestation, will allow you to feel a greater sense of control. Working on grounding yourself will allow you to have better control of your own energy so that you can exercise boundaries over what energy you are allowing to come into your personal space.

Dr. Judith Orloff has developed a 5-step plan for intuitive energy healing, which is particularly helpful for empaths. This process is essentially very similar to manifestation, as it focuses on the idea that the energy you are putting out is the energy you will attract (in this case it is intuition). The first step in this process is noticing your thoughts, beliefs, and emotions (Mason, 2005). You can look inwards through meditation or dreaming, as many of these beliefs that are negatively impacting your life can even be unconscious belief systems. Meditation is a great way to take inventory of your inner thoughts and belief systems, as is journaling, which is also a great form of creative expression.

As we've already established, problems in the body can be a sign of blocked energy in one of the chakras or meridians. Another step in healing your energy is to take inventory of your body. Taking note of how you feel throughout your body, not just in your head, can be a good indicator of where you need to focus (Mason, 2005). For instance, certain physical ailments can be a sign of an imbalanced chakra. If you feel like your throat is blocked or sore, this may signify a problem with your throat chakra. Tuning in to your physical body is a good way to notice the flow of your energy. Once you do this, you can attempt to feel your chi and the movement of energy throughout your body. A good way to start healing this is through meditation and yoga, which both increase energy flow and connect you with your source.

Orloff also suggests looking inward and asking the inner self for guidance (Mason, 2005). We can listen to our inner self and energy source by meditating, praying, connecting with nature, etc. By doing this consistently and reflecting after, specifically with certain questions or manifestations in mind, we can receive the guidance we seek from our inner source of energy. Lastly, Orloff suggests using dreams as a way to connect with your inner being and begin channeling and healing your energy. One technique to do this is by focusing on a question or intention right before you go to sleep. Then, record your dream right as you wake up, when it is still fresh in your mind. This will allow you to reflect on the unconscious answers that your brain has provided you with. By focusing on the same question or intention every night, you will find yourself healing, benefitting from the sense of control and consistency.

While these are only a few steps in a guide to intuitive healing, there are many processes that you can repeat and practice in order to tap into your intuition and start healing your energy. By grounding yourself, you will be able to really look inward and see how you are internalizing the energy around you. It is important to do this so that you can distinguish the energy that is yours authentically and the energy that you have internalized from other people. You will feel much more in control by doing this, especially if you do so consistently. Consistently looking inwards in order to take inventory of your emotions and energy may seem like a lot of effort, but once you get the hang of it, it will seem like second nature. Doing so will also benefit you greatly, allowing you to feel more focused and more in control.

Indeed, grounding exercises are very important for empaths. Empaths can often find themselves wrapped up in the energy and emotions of other people, overwhelmed and overstimulated. To avoid this, it is important to practice different grounding exercises in order to keep in touch with your inner self and intuition, and so as not to get mixed up in the emotions and energy of other people. One simple grounding technique is breathwork. You can practice this virtually anywhere, whenever you feel overwhelmed and like you need to get back in tune with your inner energy source. If you find yourself getting stressed and overwhelmed, you can start by taking a few slow breaths, counting for three seconds as you inhale and three seconds as you exhale. Repeating this five times will help you get back to the present moment and focus on the motions of your breath, which will connect you to your inner energy flow.

Another common grounding technique focuses on the senses, which for empaths are hypersensitive. Focusing on each sense as a way to ground yourself will help you be very in tune to your inner energy and the ways in which you are connected to the present moment. This technique, called the 5-4-3-2-1 technique, requires you to pay attention to your surroundings. First, take some deep breaths and then take in your surroundings, starting with identifying five things you can see. Then identify four things you can touch and feel, three sounds you can hear, two things you can smell, and one thing you can taste. Focusing on these different sensations as they relate to your surroundings is a great way to keep yourself in the present moment and avoid becoming too overwhelmed by the energy that you are taking in.

05

CHAPTER

Self-Care for Empaths

➤ Self-Care Techniques

Self-care is one of the most important steps you can take in healing as an empath. Empaths often find themselves neglecting their own needs in order to care for other people. Empaths are often the people caring for, helping and healing other people, but this can cause them to forget to heal and care for themselves. However, it is actually extremely important to prioritize their own well-being in order to effectively care for others. When we neglect our own self-care, we find ourselves less effective at our jobs and having trouble in our relationships.

Especially as an empath, being in a profession where your main job is to heal or care for others, it can be hard not to become overwhelmed by the negative energy that you are trying to heal. Furthermore, these caregivers also often spend so much time around other people that they can start to forget where their feelings end and where other people's feelings start. When you neglect your own self-care for too long, you are not yourself. In this chapter, we will go through the importance of self-care for empaths, and techniques that you can do frequently to protect your energy.

All empaths are, to an extent, high-intensity relaters. The term "high-intensity relater," coined by social worker and author Howard Brockman, refers to any person that takes on the role of a caregiver in an interpersonal context (Brockman, 2012). These people take on healing and caring for others as a job. Even if your profession does not require you to do this, as an empath you likely take on this role in many of your interpersonal relationships. While this role is what you gravitate towards and what ultimately provides you with fulfillment, it can be stressful and overwhelming. Furthermore, you will find yourself less effective in these roles if you neglect your own well-being. Just like being too selfish will negatively impact your lifestyle, you can find that being too focused on other people can actually provide you with negative consequences as well.

While this may seem contradictory, as we should all strive to be less selfish, a lack of self-awareness can also change the way you and others see yourself. Spending time caring for yourself and healing your own energy will allow you to look inwards to see how you can be more effective by working outwards. Self-care is an important priority for any human, but especially empaths. When empaths do not prioritize self-care, they can find themselves feeling lost, confused, and out of control of their emotions. Have you ever just started crying for no reason or felt very on-edge even though you did not have anything specific going on that was stressing you out? These are common things that can happen to empaths when they become stressed and overwhelmed. This is why it is important to prioritize self-care in order to prevent burnout. Even though it may seem like a lot of effort and energy at first, you will see that this direction of your energy is extremely worth it, especially in the long run.

Furthermore, doing this kind of work can make you susceptible to emotional contagion. If you do not know how to care for yourself after you have cared for others, as an empath, you can find yourself internalizing and feeling too deeply the negative trauma of others. Part of being a caregiver or healer means separating yourself, to an extent, from the issue that you are trying to work through so that you can effectively help someone else. While the ability to empathize is key to helping another person, you do not want to find yourself getting wrapped up in the distress they may be feeling, as this can have adverse effects. To keep yourself from getting into a rut due to the internalization of others' emotions, you must take care of yourself first.

Where this can sometimes get difficult for empaths is when you find yourself unconsciously internalizing the emotions of others. This is why alone time is so important for empaths. Even if you are taking measures to prioritize your own self-care, but still find yourself surrounded by other people constantly, you may still be internalizing their energy even if you are not technically "on the clock" and working as a caregiver. This is not a bad thing — as we've already established, being an empath is a gift and provides you with many spiritual and interpersonal abilities, as well as certain life skills. However, it just means that you need to make sure you are prioritizing your alone-time and recharging with self-care and in nature.

Brockman also discusses the term "compassion fatigue." This refers to symptoms that empaths and/or caregivers can suffer from when internalizing other people's pain and/or trauma too much (Brockman, 2012). It is also important that you prioritize self-care on a regular basis. If you only actively participate in activities that will help you recharge and cope with stress sporadically, you will not get into a good routine, and will likely find yourself coping with a lot of the same problems that you have been helping others work through.

After reading through this section, you might be thinking to yourself that all of this sounds very self-explanatory and straightforward. And it should seem like a basic instinct — if you are feeling down, shouldn't you do the things that make you feel better? But for empaths in particular, this is simply not as easy as it sounds. Empaths spend so much time focusing their energy and efforts on other people that they genuinely do not even think to put these healing and caregiving efforts towards themselves. Empaths can also expect to find this fulfillment in other people, choosing instead to seek the feelings of self-care in their relationships with other people, rather than in their relationship with themselves.

Empaths are also very used to putting other people's needs and feelings above their own. Because of this, they often find themselves getting pushed to the side. In our busy lives, we tend to neglect self-care as frivolous or unnecessary, when it is actually one of the most important things we can be doing. Part of this is also because we view compassion to other people and compassion to ourselves as being completely different processes, when they are inherently very similar (Barth, 2019). Self-awareness is an important aspect of this. Even though as an empath, you may believe that you are self-aware because you are focused on others, this is not inherently the case. Self-awareness can often be a casualty of being an empath, as it can even be hard to determine which emotions and energy are your own, and which are those of other people. Part of self-care is noticing which of these emotions are yours, and then intuitively acting on them. But in order to use your intuition, you must know your intuition. And this comes from self-awareness, which essentially is self-care.

Another form of self-care that researchers have studied and come to conclusions about is also related to self-compassion, which is essentially at the center of self-care. Self-compassion is the key to truly understanding your intuition and what it is you need. While the self-care that seems "fun," such as yoga or acupuncture or journaling is important and extremely beneficial, it is also important to practice the more difficult forms of self-care. This can include having hard conversations with yourself about what habits you can change and what no longer serves you. However, this can also include having these hard conversations with the people in your life. Even if it is not easy, self-care can mean cutting toxic people out of your life, such as energy vampires. If someone is taking advantage of your empathic tendencies, you may need to prioritize yourself and cut them out of your life in order to have more energy to focus on the relationships that are actually serving you. While this is hard, practicing self-compassion has countless benefits. In fact, research even shows that showing yourself compassion can work to reduce different psychological conditions and help you better handle stress (Barth, 2019).

If all of this still sounds like a foreign language to you, it's okay; we will go over a lot of different self-care techniques that you can start implementing into your routine in the next section. But if you're still wondering how you can even make self-care a main part of your routine, that's okay too. You may be thinking, "But I barely have time to eat. How am I going to find the time to meditate and do yoga every day?" But the answer to this question all comes down to priorities. You need to start putting yourself first and truly believe that self-care is the most important thing. When you really internalize and believe this, you will find all of your energy gravitating to your self-care, and making time to put yourself first will not be hard. Remember, you need to start showing yourself the same compassion that you show other people. When you start loving yourself more, you will find yourself with a greater amount of love to give to others.

Self-Care Techniques

There are endless ways to care for yourself, your body, your mind, and your spirit, and whatever forms you choose to regularly partake in are up to you. However, there are some forms of self-care that are particularly effective for empaths in particular, and some that are often recommended by doctors and therapists. Whatever forms of self-care you choose to do to de-stress and recharge, make sure you establish a solid routine and make sure to prioritize yourself on a regular basis. Consistency is key here — there is no one "right" way to care for yourself, but you will not be impressed with the results if you do not make it a priority to be consistent.

As we've already established many times throughout this book, spending time alone is a particularly effective strategy for empaths, as they often become overwhelmed and overstimulated when spending too much time around other people. Therefore, doing any activity in solitude is a great way for empaths to care for themselves, while using their intuition and getting back in tune with their own specific needs. Dr. Orloff suggests specifically not only spending time alone, but also shutting out any external stimulators that your senses are hypersensitive to. This includes turning off your TV, shutting off any bright lights, and moving away from any place where you are surrounded by other people (Orloff, 2017).

As empaths are also very energized by and find their energy being cleansed by nature, it is also a good idea to surround yourself in nature. Empaths are also recharged when around water, so going to a body of water can also be a great form of self-care. Even though empaths crave human connection, when you are prioritizing your alone time, you may find it is a good idea to shut off connection for a little while. You will find that silencing your phone and going on a walk alone will allow you to really spend time with your thoughts. This, in turn, will let you distinguish your true energy source, and you can use your intuition to get in touch with your thoughts and feelings without any distracting energy from others. This will also make your manifestations more effective, as you will be focusing on your beliefs, feelings, and what you desire, rather than the feelings of other people around you.

Another form of self-care for empaths that can be incorporated into your daily life is boundary-setting. This is an essential life skill for anyone, not just empaths, but is extremely important to protect your energy from emotional contagion and "energy vampires" (Orloff, 2017). Setting boundaries on when and how you communicate will allow you to prioritize and protect your personal well-being from those who may be taking advantage of you. Even though you are a helper at heart, when you give too much to others and allow them to burden you too much, this can negatively affect every aspect of your life. At its most extreme, you can find yourself so burdened that you suffer emotionally, mentally, and even physically. And when you are suffering, you cannot be an effective caregiver or healer to others. Think about how you can easily notice when there is something wrong with someone close to you — they can notice this in you, too.

For this reason, it is extremely important that you make yourself, your well-being, and your intuition your top priorities. If this means distancing yourself for a time and setting boundaries, then it is necessary to take these actions in order to ultimately benefit everyone. It may not seem like setting boundaries is a form of self-care since it often involves your relationships with other people. However, since empaths are so relationship-focused, self-care definitely does involve creating healthy boundaries and habits within your relationships. You can start doing this gradually, by setting clear intentions about what it is you feel is important to prioritize. Once you start setting boundaries, you will get into the habit of doing this in your relationships and you will be able to see the benefits.

One of the most important factors in your well-being is something you have probably heard time and time again: get enough sleep. Sleep is the way that we truly "recharge." Even if you are following all the other tips in this book, if you are not getting enough sleep, you are not going to be balanced and healthy. This is science — sleep will help you stay your healthiest physically, mentally, and spiritually. According to Orloff, a lack of sleep can even cause you to absorb more negative energy. Have you ever found yourself to be much more on-edge and susceptible to absorbing negative energy when you are deprived of much-needed rest? It is a proven fact that we do not perform as well as we could, in anything, when we are not getting enough sleep.

Additionally, sleep can have many benefits as they relate to dreaming and energy healing. The more you sleep, the more you dream. This heals your energy, soul, and physical health, which is self-care in its most traditional sense. If you are feeling out of sorts and stressed out, there are also many guided sleep meditations you can listen to as you close your eyes that will help your brain unconsciously heal your energy while you sleep. Remember, the average adult needs 7-8 hours of sleep a night. This form of self-care (as with all forms of self-care) is not a luxury, but a necessity. If you are not sleeping enough, you are not doing one of the most basic things you can do to protect your overall well-being.

Another great self-care technique, specifically for empaths, is journaling. Journaling is an amazing and therapeutic way to express your emotions and creativity. It will also allow you to really tap into your intuition, as by writing down everything and anything that comes to mind, you are validating and noticing where your thoughts and energy lie. Journaling is also an effective tool for manifestation. By writing down what you hope to manifest, this can help you visualize what it is you want and how you will feel when you have attracted this thing. It also validates what you are attempting to manifest, and it solidifies that relation to the universe as you seek to attract that feeling. For empaths specifically, journaling is a great way to work through and identify any emotions you may be confused about.

Another great self-care technique to increase your positive energy flow is expressing gratitude. This can be done with journaling or meditation and is essential to manifestation. By focusing on everything in your life that you are grateful for, you will find that you will start looking at your situation in a more positive light, and whatever may be causing you stress will no longer seem quite as bad. By expressing gratitude, you can improve a mindset that may have turned negative due to energy vampires or emotional contagion.

Another type of self-care that can specifically benefit empaths or other highly sensitive people is going to therapy. Since empaths are generally the "therapists," in their relationships, being the ones that other people go to for advice and problem-solving, a lot of their own problems and trauma may get swept under the rug. Therefore, seeing a professional can be extremely beneficial, even If It Just provides you with someone to talk to. Therapists are also helpful in providing us with tools and resources to work through any mental disorders we may suffer from. Going to therapy is a great way to unpack any pent-up emotional trauma so that you can stop being weighed down by stress and negative emotions that you may be internalizing from the people around you. Therapy is proven to benefit your interpersonal relationships and problem-solving skills, so if you are really struggling with carrying the weight that empaths often carry, reaching out to a professional could be good for you.

Furthermore, as an empath, you may be prone to attracting energy vampires who consistently talk your ear off and unload their baggage onto you. By going to therapy, you can lighten this load a little bit, freeing up space to work on your own intuitive energy. You can also find that it becomes easier for you to work on your intuitive gifts, as you have more energy to focus on the things that matter to you. When you start unpacking your inner emotions, you will find that a lot of doors open up for you.

You can also incorporate self-care into your routine in the form of practicing spirituality in order to benefit both your body and mind. Self-care includes tuning in to your physical well-being and seeing where you can improve. Exercise is a great way to clear your mind and release stress, as not only does it benefit your body, but it releases endorphins, improving and clearing your energy. Another form of self-care is balancing your chakras, which you will benefit from physically, spiritually, and emotionally.

You can even incorporate many of these techniques into your sleep. By listening to different guided sleep meditations as you doze off, you can clear your energy while you are asleep, waking up refreshed and energized in the morning. You can, of course, focus on different spiritual practices that work for you. For example, you may find that you hate meditation, but you love doing yoga. Whichever practices you think promote your wellness in the best way possible, make sure to practice them as often as you can and really build a routine. Just how working out once a month will simply not be as effective as regularly building a workout routine a few times a week, you must do the same with your spirituality in order to truly see the benefits.

While these are only a few self-care techniques for empaths specifically, there are a multitude of other ways you can regularly take some time for yourself to recharge. Whatever works for you, you will find that it improves the flow of your energy within and without your spirit and body. In these next sections, we will focus on how you can apply the idea of self-care specifically to different energy forms and healing. Healing is an important part of the self-care process. We cannot heal our energy without prioritizing ourselves, and this may mean feeling like you are putting certain parts of your life on hold. But remember, when you put yourself first, you will see that all of your relationships will end up benefiting in return. By prioritizing yourself, you are actually prioritizing your relationships with other people because you are learning how to deliver your best self.

06

CHAPTER

How to Re-Channel Your Energy

➤ Why and How Should We Learn to Redirect Energy?

Now that we've discussed the importance of prioritizing self-care, you may have decided that you're ready to start refocusing your energy into your own personal well-being. But you may also be thinking to yourself that this is probably much easier said than done, and that is a valid point. Re-channeling energy to yourself that you've been directing into other people for your whole life is not an easy feat. Energy healing is a process — it is not something that comes easy, and it takes a lot of work and practice to learn how to truly tap into our energy sources and direct it into our own personal well-being.

Empaths tend to neglect themselves, instead directing all of their energy to other people. But by directing some of your energy into healing yourself, you will actually tap into a source of true abundance. Rather than wearing yourself thin, as empaths tend to do, you will find that you have an abundance of love and joy to give out. The key to accessing this energy and using your intuitive gifts is simply accessing and redirecting this energy source, which we will learn how to do in the next chapters. But first, let's talk a little bit more about what energy healing actually is. We've already discussed meridians and chakras and how they dictate the flow of energy, and we've established what chi is. But now let's define how some of the processes behind actually healing the body's energy flow work.

One popular holistic form of energy healing, as an alternative psychiatric healing form, is Reiki energy healing. Reiki energy healing is a holistic treatment that works to heal the mind, body, and spirit. As we've established, a lot of the ways in which our energy flows throughout our body not only depend on the mind but on the physical being as well. Reiki healing, which was discovered by a Japanese man, focuses on this connection (Green Lotus, 2011). The healing form focuses on the flows of energy in the body that are blocked or have been turned negative, and heals them, turning them positive (Reiki Administration, 2014).

As an empath, this practice can be particularly beneficial as it helps to release internalized negative energy. Empaths find all too often that they have unintentionally internalized negative energy from other people. While non-empaths are able to be more selective over the energy that comes into their bodies, simply because they are less sensitive to stimulants, empaths internalize other people's emotions and energy at a much higher frequency. Reiki healing works specifically to raise the vibrations surrounding the points of negative energy in the body, helping an empath release a lot of these emotions that they have unintentionally internalized.

Reiki also works to reduce stress and feelings of pain by increasing relaxation, ultimately raising the vibrations around the body. It also seeks to clear any energy blockages in the body, which allows energy to flow more freely within and without. This applies holistic treatment and energy balance to the body (Green Lotus, 2011). Reiki healing, though once not regarded as an actual medical treatment, has now been studied quite extensively and is even offered at some hospitals. If you are looking to receive Reiki healing, you can likely find a local provider near you, since it is a medical as well as holistic practice.

Another popular and commonly used form of energy healing is Pranic healing. This form of energy healing differs from Reiki healing in that it does not take a hands-on approach to healing the body's energy flows. Instead, Pranic healing holds the belief that the body can heal itself through different methods based on whatever health ailment one is suffering from. Pranic healing holds the belief system that our energy source, which is referred to as Prana, flows within and without the body, and that our body can fix any blockages that might result (*Intro to Pranic Healing, n.d.*). This healing method focuses on different areas of the body's energy field that might be affected by a blockage. For instance, if you were to go in to see a pranic healer with a problem affecting your lower back or the base of your spine, the healer would likely focus on your root chakra and attempt to heal the energy that flows in this area of the energy field.

Both forms of energy healing are widely popularized, though they have different methods. There are also countless other energy healing methods, and selecting the right one for you will take self-awareness and will depend on your personal goals. However, there are also ways in which you can work to balance your own energy flows, which we will explore in the next sections.

Why And How Should We Learn To Redirect Energy?

While we've discussed some popular forms of professional energy healing, there are also ways in which you can work to redirect the negative energy in your body yourself. The first step in this process involves actively and intuitively noticing when you are internalizing negative energy around you. As an empath, you likely already have a strong intuition. However, it can sometimes be difficult to tell when an emotion is naturally yours and when it is someone else's. Therefore, you might need to take some time alone to meditate on your thoughts, feelings, and intentions to determine how you need to heal your own energy. It is important to remain conscious and aware of how your energy is affecting your mood and your life. Since empaths are so susceptible to internalizing energy around them without even realizing it, it is extra important to remain conscious and self-aware. This is why journaling and meditation are great tools for remaining in touch with your specific energy field and the processes going on in your mind and body. These actions allow you to observe your thoughts and the energy flowing through you.

In order to start to cleanse your energy and free up any blockages in general, without focusing on any specific points, you must first sit with and notice your thoughts.

Meditating or spending time alone in nature will help you to do this. Your thoughts can represent the flow of energy throughout your body, as the thoughts that you find yourself focusing on the most are the things that you are giving the most energy. This, in turn, attracts more of whatever you are focusing on, as the Law of Attraction tells us that the thoughts that you give the most energy to become the things that you attract into your life.

You must also examine your personal belief systems. What are you focusing on, and what is no longer serving you at this current moment? Noticing what exactly it is that your energy is applied to will help you learn how to heal it. You also need to focus on being conscious and aware — this can often be difficult for empaths, as their first instinct is to put all of their focus onto the emotions of others. However, with practice, you can develop attention to your inner movement rather than outer stimulants. It is precisely a lack of conscious awareness that will worsen an energy imbalance, so awareness is the first step in healing this.

If you are still having trouble pinpointing where you should be trying to redirect the energy in your life, try thinking about different aspects of it. Maybe you feel like you never have a day off work and are constantly working overtime, yet you still seem to be broke. In this case, your energy might be blocked as it relates to abundance in your life. You can also use the Law of Attraction and manifestation techniques to enhance your energy healing. But by focusing on the lack of wealth you have, that is what you are attracting into your life. In order to start healing the way your energy flows, it is important to express gratitude and start framing things from a positive light. Instead of focusing on the feeling of lacking money, focus on the gratitude you have for your job and the chance to earn money. You will find that this heals the negative energy surrounding this aspect of your life. You can apply this to different areas of your life, even your relationships. It is also important that, as an empath, you examine the way energy flows through your different interpersonal relationships. Do you have any relationships which you believe you are the only one putting energy in, yet you still end up with negative feelings about the relationship? This may be a sign that you need to reexamine who and what really deserves your time and energy.

It is important to always remain mindful of what we are putting our energy into. However, if we find that this does not serve us, we can start learning to redirect where we are channeling our energy. As an empath, this may be difficult to understand, since an empath's first instinct is to direct all of their energy into understanding and helping others. However, this is counterintuitive to your own healing, and this can actually make you the type of negative person that you are seeking to avoid. Distancing yourself from this negative energy is a great form of self-care, and you will see the positive effects. There are also many measures you can take to protect your own energy from any toxic influences. This will allow you to monitor any patterns you have noticed so as not to hinder your personal growth.

How To Prevent And Heal Energy Blockages

Now that we've discussed some techniques for clearing energy blockages, let's backtrack and discuss how our energy can even become "blocked." Some signs of energy blockage may be so common to you that you don't even realize how truly significant they are. One common sign that your energy flow is blocked is finding that your thoughts are stuck. This is also a common symptom of an anxiety disorder, and empaths can often struggle with this. Having thoughts that are stuck or fixed on one thing, and finding yourself unable to think about anything else or get your mind off the subject, can indicate a blockage in this area of your life.

Why can't you stop your mind from gravitating to this one area of your life? It is important to figure out what it is that will allow you to get "unstuck," even if you are not there yet. Once you can imagine what it is that would take your mind off this fixed thought, you can recreate the feeling of it. For instance, maybe you are worried about a test you just took and cannot seem to stop thinking about it, even though you already turned it in. You know that you would stop worrying about the test if you got a good grade on it. So, in order to get "unstuck" from this unnecessary waste of energy, imagine the feeling you would have when you found out you got a good grade on this test. Then, internalize this feeling and replace your anxious feelings about the test with this positive feeling.

You can also focus on the energy flow throughout each specific chakra. If you know that as an empath you may be prone to energy blocks in your heart chakra, then it would be a good idea to implement ways to prioritize self-care that will directly affect your heart chakra. Furthermore, as we will explore in the next chapter, you may still be feeling the effects of previous trauma that has built up and never fully been resolved. When you don't fully prioritize healing and clear this blocked energy, the places where you experience blockages will just be reinforced and continue to impact your life in different ways. This can even impact the flows of positive energy in other areas of your life.

It may also be hard for you to distinguish where you have blocked energy since you are so susceptible to internalizing the energy of others. While this can also create blocks, these blockages are not necessarily the same as energetic and emotional blockages that result from pent up and unhealed trauma. In order to start prioritizing your healing process, it is important for you to examine the areas of your life that you are not fully content with. Do you find yourself constantly repeating the same bad habits, even though you consciously want to break them? These bad habits can manifest in the forms of procrastination, purposely sabotaging relationships, and even over-eating.

A good way to start healing your blocked energy is by creating a list of all the areas in your life that do not seem to have free-flowing, positive energy. Maybe you even feel that you can sometimes be close-minded to new ideas — why do you think this is? By pinpointing the areas in which pent up emotional trauma has most affected you, you can begin to effectively heal. Some of these blockages can even impact your physical health and well-being, as we've established that different chakras are focused in different areas of the body.

A good tool to work on preventing energy blockages and heal any aspects that you think might be blocked is crystal healing. This is another popular form of alternative medicine, as it is believed that different crystals have different effects on our energy flows. It is believed that crystals improve energy flows throughout our body and can help rid the body of any pent-up negative energy. Different crystals provide different functions and can be used in different ways to help prevent energy blockages. For instance, if you seek to improve the flow of love in your life and often find you have trouble in relationships, you may want to meditate with a rose quartz stone or keep it by your bed while you sleep. If you want to ward off negative energy from entering your energy field, as can often happen to empaths, you may find it useful to start meditating with and keeping citrine. This stone will allow you to protect your balanced, positive energy from external threats to your inner peace.

There are also many techniques for empaths, in particular, to prevent toxic and negative energy from entering their mind and body. One great way to do this is by boundary-setting. Boundary-setting is often not in the nature of empaths, as they naturally seek closeness with others and enjoy being healers and/or caregivers. However, doing this is extremely important to protect your own energy. Think of it as creating a protective barrier around your energy field — you do not want toxins to have the ability to freely come in and contaminate everything around them. By looking at where in your relationships you can start creating healthy boundaries, you will find that you project much more positive energy, which is what you will attract in return. This also likely goes without saying, but energy can easily be protected through engaging in more self-care. When you become more in tune with your thoughts, emotions, and intuition, it becomes more difficult for negative energy to permeate your spirit.

Another strong form of protecting your energy flows is by teaching yourself to notice energy without initially reacting to it. This can often be practiced in meditation, as you notice a thought and then simply let it go without reacting or responding to it. Your first instinct may often be to respond to stimuli, trying to always help people when you feel that you can. However, it is important to first take note of how energy and emotions are impacting you. Keeping track of what energy is flowing around you and how you are internalizing it is key to choosing how you can best respond when you choose to do so. As empaths can often think with their hearts and not their heads, they may often impulsively act on emotions. However, by keeping track and truly noticing the flow of your emotions and energy, and what is causing certain reactions in you, you will feel much more in control of your own energy patterns.

Another way in which you can prevent energy blockages is by shifting your mindset as it relates to other people. As an empath, you obviously want to help others. But do you ever feel as if you are trying to change them or help them solve problems in vain? You may have to cope with the fact that some people just are the way they are. An overinvestment in other people could result in less satisfaction for everyone, as you could feel as if no progress is being made, and they could feel that you are unfairly trying to change them. Letting go of your expectations of other people is a great way to start redirecting your energy into your own intuition and well-being. This is also an unproductive way to seek control. While empaths often do strive to gain control of their lives and situations, trying to control the feelings, emotions, and behaviors of other people is never beneficial for anyone. Instead, control the ways in which you are reacting to and internalizing their emotions. You can also gain this sense of control over your energy by focusing inwards. Although you cannot control the fact that you are naturally an empath, you can control the ways you respond to other people's energy and emotions. By strengthening your own sense of intuition, you will find the control that you crave.

And remember, there is no energy healing without self-care. The two go hand-in-hand, and if you want to start improving the way your energy flows and redirect what your attention goes to, you must start prioritizing self-care. Through doing this, you will be able to discover your unconscious thoughts and emotions, which may surprise you. This also might be hard at first, but it will eventually be extremely worth it, and you will reap the benefits in every aspect of your life.

07

CHAPTER

Healing as an Empath

➤ Common Traumas That Empaths
Experience

Although we have already discussed many different forms of energy healing, it is important to wrap up this guide on tapping into your intuition by acknowledging the importance of cherishing and nurturing your intuitive gifts. As we've already established, many empaths find that their natural intuitive gifts have been suppressed or made to lie dormant due to a lack of encouragement in our culture. This, combined with the possible trauma you could face from the constant internalization of other people's negative energy and emotions, could result in feelings of helplessness or hopelessness. However, it is possible to heal. Choosing to read this book and actively pay more attention to your inner energy source and intuition is the first step in healing these gifts. By noticing where you can improve the flows of energy in your life, you are taking an important first step towards prioritizing your own well-being and putting yourself first. Now, let's discuss some common traumas you may find yourself especially susceptible to as an empath.

Dr. Orloff suggests that one of the first steps to healing is to identify what kind of an empath you believe yourself to be (Orloff, 2018). Are you more of a physical or emotional empath? Orloff defines a physical empath as being someone who is more in tune to the physical feelings of others, and that is how they connect with others' energy sources. For instance, the "super empaths" that we discussed earlier in this book would qualify as physical empaths. Physical empaths are typically able to physically internalize the feelings of others. For instance, if a friend is suffering from a physical ailment, an empath may internally be able to feel some of this pain in their own body (Orloff, 2018). However, this also means that when someone feels physically well, physical empaths can pick up on that well-being also.

Conversely, an emotional empath feels the emotions of other people almost as deeply as the primary feeler does. This seems to be more common in empaths. For instance, many people can feel great about their own life, but if they spend time with someone who radiates negative emotions, they can find themselves internalizing these negative emotions as if they were their own. This is why it is incredibly important to learn how to protect your own energy so that you are at less risk of feeling the negative effects of other people's trauma and emotions. Emotional empaths also often struggle with differentiating the overlap between their emotions and other people's emotions (Orloff, 2017). However, this does not mean that as an empath, you have to cut other people out of your life simply because they are sad. Rather, it means that you can just start to work on protecting your own energy so that you can maintain a strong relationship without necessarily allowing their negativity to permeate your energy field.

One strong way to start healing your energy from any invading forces is not only setting boundaries, but actually using the Law of Attraction as well as visualization in order to really keep your energy safe from the energy of those close to you. It is important to first look inwards and actually examine where your emotions and thoughts start, and where those of other people end. You can then actually visualize yourself setting up a boundary around your energy, and in a sense severing energetic ties with the energy fields of others. By manifesting this, you can still express empathy without feeling exactly what other people are feeling to the same degree.

A simple exercise to do this is by first taking deep breaths, calming yourself, and focusing on the flow of your breath. Think of this like meditation, as you are trying to get yourself into that calm, focused headspace. You can then start envisioning yourself creating a protective forcefield around yourself in order to keep your energy safe from outside forces. You can also visualize yourself cutting energetic ties with another person in order to stop their energy from affecting you as much as it does. You can imagine your energies being connected by a rope and that you are cutting this rope with scissors. These visualization exercises will be very helpful in allowing you to ground yourself and maintain your energetic integrity.

There are many ways in which you can unlearn toxic behaviors that may have been developed as a result of trauma, as well as develop new coping and healing mechanisms to help you move forward. However, the first step to doing this is to unpack what it is that has caused you trauma so that you can discover how to best heal. Healing trauma related to a fear of being different as compared to trauma from a toxic relationship will be a different process. By pinpointing where your trauma derives from and how it is currently impacting your energy flows, you can start to notice where these energy blocks come from and how you can fix them. Doing this will be a great first step on your journey to healing as an empath. You can start by journaling and meditating. Doing a grounding meditation is a great way to get in touch with your inner thoughts and feelings, especially the ones that you may not notice at a surface level. By paying attention to how you feel and how your energy seems to be flowing throughout different sectors of your life, you can gain a lot of insight into what you can work on and what is no longer serving you.

Furthermore, empaths can start internalizing trauma that comes from toxic relationships. Empaths are essentially magnets for energy vampires looking to take advantage of them. This can take a great toll on their well-being, as the relationship-related trauma can manifest itself as difficulties in other relationships. However, there are ways to heal in our relationships. It is possible not only to ground yourself and start healing yourself from within, but you can also have conversations with those close to you about trauma you may be going through in order to heal together. You can start to examine your relationships, and see how the energy is flowing in each of them. The first place to look is if you have any relationships with energy vampires at the current moment. One symptom of pent-up trauma is that you can find yourself repeating the habit of starting relationships with energy vampires over and over again, subconsciously allowing them to permeate your energy field and take advantage of you. As we've established, the first step to healing in this regard is through self-reflection. Self-reflection and the exercise of your empathic intuitive gifts will ultimately be the best way for you to start to heal.

Common Traumas That Empaths Experience

There are many traumatic experiences that empaths are particularly prone to. However, by understanding and noticing what these kinds of trauma may be, you are well positioned on the path to healing. It is important to make a list of anything you feel might be a problem with your energy. Do you find that you get particularly anxious in social settings and have a hunch that you might be prone to social anxiety? Take note of that. Do you also notice that when being around someone sad, you internalize feelings of depression that can worsen your own emotions? Take note of that as well. Empaths are often very prone to social anxiety because of how sensitive they are to stimuli. They can pick up on the most subtle energies, noticing things that other people may not notice. Because of this, empaths can become very easily stressed and overwhelmed in social settings, especially as children when they are just learning to use their intuition and likely do not understand their gifts (Orloff, 2018). This is one common trauma that empaths face, as being in large groups of people and in crowds can be overwhelming and stimulating to the point of avoidance.

Another common trauma for empaths is fear of rejection (Orloff, 2018). Empaths are ultimately people that crave emotional connection with other people. When they feel as if they are being rejected, this can impact them much more deeply and impactfully than non-empaths. Even if it is a non-personal rejection, such as a lost job opportunity, empaths can often find themselves feeling the effects of rejection to their deepest extent. This can be another instance of when empaths are accused of being "too sensitive," or seeming to take things further than expected. The reason for this, however, is just that empaths deeply crave emotional connection, and rejection feels like a refusal of that.

Another unique form of trauma that empaths may be affected by beyond childhood is the feeling that they are not truly being themselves, or that they are living out of fear of not being accepted. This can come from many years of teaching themselves to suppress their emprathic abilities, which can show up in adulthood as having a fear of truly being yourself or as closing yourself off emotionally. In order to move past this, it is necessary to get back in touch with your intuition and energy source to start tapping back into your natural gifts and emotions. There are many healing techniques that can be done to accomplish this.

Another source of trauma for empaths can be their relationships with people who drain them of their energy, or energy vampires. These people can cause empaths to feel taken advantage of, drained, and generally cause them to absorb a great deal of negative energy. This can also be a form of an abusive relationship. Emotionally abusive relationships can create a source of unhealed trauma for empaths, causing them to have trouble forming new connections and succeeding in future relationships. This is another area in which it is important to focus on redirecting and healing your energy flows as they relate to other people.

Many empaths can often become empaths as a result of abuse they may have faced as children. This can be something extremely difficult that they then have to work through in adulthood. For instance, some empaths are hypersensitive to even the slightest changes in other people, which is actually how they were ultimately able to tell if they were in danger. While this skill of sensing danger is a benefit of being an empath, being abused can be the unfortunate reason behind their developing this skill. Therefore, this trauma can carry over into their later life, causing empaths to find themselves very on-edge and hypersensitive to anything they believe could be a danger to them, even if it is not. This can be a sort of "side-effect" of being an empath and explains a lot of why empaths can seem more reserved or closed-off to other people, simply because they are very sensitive to possible threats. Empaths can also develop what is perceived as paranoia because of this. Even though they are oftentimes right about their intuition, it can be written off as paranoia because they are the first to sense the true and subtle energy of a person or situation. This can also cause them to somewhat suppress their natural intuition, not wanting to trust it for fear of being paranoid, which can manifest in adulthood as unhealed trauma.

Another common trauma that empaths experience, due to a lack of grounding and healing, is the tendency to absorb all the emotions around them. This can cause them to feel taken for granted, or that they are letting people walk all over them. When they consistently let toxic people take them for granted and drain them of energy, especially earlier in life, this can reinforce a feeling of helplessness later in life. Empaths can often find that they have trouble sticking up for themselves or saying no to people, simply because of habits they created as children. However, by working on setting boundaries and grounding yourself, you can protect your own energy enough to where you are able to know what should and should not be entering your energetic field.

As we've already discussed, having empathic gifts can also be a gateway to self-destructive patterns, such as consistently entering toxic relationships and addiction. Empaths often find that they seek to "numb the pain" that comes with being an empath. This can result in destructive behaviors, as they are unable to cope with the feelings of constantly being overstimulated. This is why self-care is so important for empaths. It is imperative that they find outlets through which they can channel and express emotions, both their own and others, so as not to feel overwhelmed and distraught by the weight that they carry.

Healing Techniques For Empaths

While there are quite a few common patterns that can block the energy of an empath, there are a number of tools and techniques you can use to heal your energy. One great strategy is definitely easier than it sounds — noticing and taking inventory of your thoughts and emotions as you feel them. This is so much easier said than done, as no one wants to actively be thinking about every thought they have, analyzing why and how they are feeling each emotion that crosses their mind. However, you can consciously build these actions into your self-care routine. Try to take more time for yourself to meditate and reflect on the thoughts you are having. It is also a great idea to journal with the intention of differentiating your feelings and the feelings of others. Putting your thoughts into perspective and analyzing what it is that makes you feel the way you do is a great way to bring a sense of control and balance back into your body. This perspective will allow you to remain empathic, but you likely will not be as deeply impacted by others' emotions when you are putting conscious awareness into how they impact your mind.

As another strategy for healing energy caused by the trauma of internalizing others' emotions, Orloff suggests repeating the mantra 'return to sender' (Orloff, 2018). When repeating this mantra, it is important to also focus on the flow of your breath, inhaling and exhaling slowly as you repeat the mantra either aloud or in your head. This mantra works to release any negative energy that you have internalized from those around you. By confidently repeating this mantra, you can direct the energy out of your body. This is a great technique to do when you have been around a large group of people, or if you simply just find yourself feeling a little bit "off." By directing this toxic energy out of your mind and body, you will be better able to focus on the energy that has originated from you.

Another way to reduce the inflow of toxic and traumatic energy, particularly for physical empaths, is to increase your physical distance. If you are in a crowded place and feeling out of control of the toxic energies you are internalizing, you can physically step away and take some time to recharge. It is important for you to normalize doing this in group settings and crowded places, particularly if you hold trauma related to being in large groups. Many empaths can find that they have trauma specifically related to spending too much time with large groups as a child. Another way that you can increase your physical distance is by reducing physical contact with other people. Since energy is often transferred through physical touch, if you feel that you need to heal your energy and protect your body from internalizing too much toxic external energy, you can make the choice to reduce physical contact with other people, specifically those you are not as close too (Orloff, 2018).

You can also increase your distance on an emotional level. As we've already established, healing pent-up trauma can often be accomplished by setting boundaries and limits on interpersonal communication. It is perfectly valid to decide that you need and/or want space from other individuals. If one of your friends is burdening you with energy that reminds you of a past traumatic incident, it is perfectly valid to take some time to distance yourself so that you can heal and separate your energy from theirs.

It's also important to allow yourself solitary time to regroup and truly focus on healing. Even if you feel as if you consciously are prioritizing your self-care, it is important to actually commit to healing. This can mean unlearning past tendencies of codependency. For instance, empaths often find themselves becoming codependent in their relationships, which can actually result in more problems with closeness. If you are someone that does not know how to comfortably be alone and spend time with yourself, this is probably a result of past trauma you've developed from different empathic characteristics. You can start by sitting alone with your thoughts for just a small amount of time. Spending time in nature is also a great way to recharge and heal your energy from the effects of trauma.

Remember to also try visualization. You can practice some different grounding techniques that will help you focus your energy on grounding yourself and being in touch with your own energy. Unlearning trauma is not an easy feat. It is hard and can take a lot of time and energy to consciously focus on unlearning trauma, but it is worth it to work through any energetic blocks you may encounter.

Conclusion

Now that we've discussed many of the qualities of empaths, you may be finding that you think of yourself as an empath, even if you had not previously considered the possibility. You may also find that you are not an empath, but do identify as a very empathetic person. Either way, it is important to take steps to ground yourself and make sure that you protect your energy from any influences that could be harmful to you. You can also use the tips and tricks mentioned earlier to start tapping into your intuition and the gifts that being an empath provides you with. As you have read throughout this book, being an empath allows you to have a keen sense of inner intuition that allows you to pick up on even the most subtle energetic changes. This often proves itself to be a huge gift, as you are able to excel at things like energy healing, manifestation, and even different clairvoyant activities.

By reading this book, you hopefully have learned how to become more in tune with your own energy and thoughts. While being an empath allows you to be very skilled at picking up on the energy and emotions of others, the most important thing is that you learn how to apply this to yourself. You must focus on looking inwards to discover how you can protect your own energy and emotions from those of other people. Doing this will allow you to apply your empathic gifts more successfully. This personality type is often seen as a gift, although it can be overwhelming and seem as if there are many setbacks that come with it. With all the constant overstimulation that you might find yourself susceptible to, especially with social media, you may find that you are unable to ever truly recharge. The constant stimulation that you find yourself taking in via social media, the news, and different social interactions can be especially draining to empaths, and you must learn to protect yourself from these stimulators.

It is understandable to become drained and overwhelmed, but as we've discussed, there are many different steps you can take in order to ground yourself and focus on redirecting your energy. The key to maintaining your own energetic integrity is to focus on channeling it into yourself and to focus on prioritizing self-care and boundary setting in order to avoid the influx of negative energy that you would otherwise take in. You can also focus on the gifts that come with being an empath. Instead of allowing yourself to become wrapped up in the energetic problems that you face, focus instead on applying your intuitive gifts. You can use the tools of manifestation and meditation to attract virtually anything into your life — this is a gift! Because you are an empath, you will also find that this gift comes very naturally to you. You can use the tools that have been outlined earlier in order to focus your energy on your specific energetic gifts. Remember to focus on grounding yourself through meditation and nature. By doing this, you will avoid some of the feelings of being out of control that empaths can often face. This will allow you to channel your energy into what really matters, such as improving yourself and your intuition.

Because of the tendency to become overstimulated so easily, we must make sure that we maintain a healthy balance of self-care in our everyday routine in order to avoid becoming burned out and overwhelmed. Remember to focus on noticing emotions and energy first before reacting to them. Empaths often find that they have difficulty with reacting right away, or even not knowing how to react, which can result in many difficulties for them in their relationships. This can also result in an overload of emotions, which can cause difficulties in different aspects of life. However, when you empower yourself to heal your energy and work through any pent-up emotions, you will find that you can thrive as an empath.

References

➤ American College of Neuropsychopharmacology. (2018, December 10). Why feeling empathy could lead former drug users to relapse: Empathy and addiction.

ScienceDaily. www.sciencedaily.com/releases/2018/12/181210072543.htm

➤ Barth, F. D. (2019). Self-Care Is Important: Why Is It So Hard to Practice?

Psychology Today. https://www.psychologytoday.com/us/blog/the-couch/201905/self-care-is-important-why-is-it-so-hard-practice

➤ Brockman, H. (2012). Essential self-care for caregivers & helpers - preserve your health, maintain your well-being, and create effective boundaries. Columbia Press.

➤ Decety, J., & Moriguchi, Y. (2007). The empathic brain and its dysfunction in psychiatric populations: implications for intervention across different clinical conditions.

BioPsychoSocial Medicine, 1(1), 22. https://doi.org/10.1186/1751-0759-1-22

➤ Green Lotus, (2011). Reiki Really Works: A Groundbreaking Scientific Study A Brief Explanation of Reiki.

https://www.uclahealth.org/rehab/workfiles/urban%20zen/research%20articles/reiki_really_works-a_groundbreaking_scientific_study.pdf

➤ Intro to Pranic Healing. (n.d.). Master Co. Retrieved June 20, 2020, from

https://www.masterco.org/intro-pranic-healing

➤ Mason, R. (2005). The Energy Psychiatry of Judith Orloff, M.D. Alternative and Complementary Therapies, 11(1), 32–36.

https://doi.org/10.1089/act.2005.11.32

➤ Melchers, M. C., Li, M., Haas, B. W., Reuter, M., Bischoff, L., & Montag, C. (2016). Similar Personality Patterns Are Associated with Empathy in Four Different Countries.

Frontiers in Psychology, 7. https://doi.org/10.3389/fpsyg.2016.00290

➤ Meridian Connection | TCM World. (2019). TCM World.

https://www.tcmworld.org/what-is-tcm/meridian-connection/

➤ Orloff, J., M.D. (2017). EMPATHY TO A FAULT. Alternative Medicine, (34), 44-46.

Retrieved from https://search.proquest.com/docview/1913308531?accountid=14696

➤ Orloff, J. (2018). The empath's survival guide : life strategies for sensitive people. Sounds True, Inc.

➤ Orloff, J. (2017, March 3). The Science Behind Empathy and Empaths.

Psychology Today. https://www.psychologytoday.com/us/blog/the-empaths-survival-guide/201703/the-science-behind-empathy-and-empaths

➤ Reiki Administrator. (2014, October 15). How Does Reiki Work? Reiki.

https://www.reiki.org/faqs/how-does-reiki-work

➤ Riess, H. (2017). The Science of Empathy. Journal of Patient Experience, 4(2), 74–77.

https://doi.org/10.1177/2374373517699267

➤ Smolewska, K. (2006). A psychometric evaluation of the highly sensitive person scale: The components of sensory-processing sensitivity and their relation to the BIS/BAS and "Big five" (Order No. MR23771). Available from ProQuest Dissertations & Theses Global. (304907170).

https://search.proquest.com/docview/304907170?accountid=14696

➤ "Super empaths" with rare condition can feel your pain - Economic and Social Research Council. (2018, November 13).

Esrc.Ukri.Org. https://esrc.ukri.org/news-events-and-publications/news/news-items/super-empaths-with-rare-condition-can-feel-your-pain/

➤ The Hazards of Being an Empath. (2020, January 18).

Promises Behavioral Health. https://www.promisesbehavioralhealth.com/addiction-recovery-blog/the-hazards-of-being-an-empath/

➤ The Psychology of Emotional and Cognitive Empathy | Lesley University. (2019).

Lesley.Edu. https://lesley.edu/article/the-psychology-of-emotional-and-cognitive-empathy

➤ What Is Spirituality? | Taking Charge of Your Health & Wellbeing. (2019). Taking Charge of Your Health & Wellbeing.

https://www.takingcharge.csh.umn.edu/what-spirituality

Image References

➤ Altmann, G. (2014). Thinking Consideration.

In Pixabay. https://pixabay.com/illustrations/judge-consider-thinking-300551/

➤ Altmann, G. (2015). Empathy Head Outlines.

In Pixabay. https://pixabay.com/illustrations/face-head-empathy-meet-sensitivity-985964/

➤ Altmann, G. (2019). Brainwave awareness.

In Pixabay. https://pixabay.com/illustrations/brain-wave-awareness-compassion-4372151/

➤ Caliskan, O. (2019). Spiritual Awakening Chakra.

In Pixabay. https://pixabay.com/photos/spiritualism-awakening-meditation-4552237/

➤ Chiplanay. (2020). Yoga in the Moonlight.

In Pixabay. https://pixabay.com/illustrations/relax-yoga-meditate-relajacion-5158376/

➤ Chomotovski, A. (2017). Sunrise Woman Silhouette.

In Pixabay. https://pixabay.com/photos/morning-sunrise-woman-silhouette-2243465/

➤ Crescoli, G. (2017). Smiley Emoticons.

In Pixabay. https://pixabay.com/photos/smiley-emoticon-anger-angry-2979107/

➤ Hain, J. (2015). Silhouette with Text and Emojis.

In Pixabay. https://pixabay.com/illustrations/transformation-emoji-mystery-spirit-857734/

➤ Henseler, K. (2020). Relaxing Meditation with Chakra.

In Pixabay. https://pixabay.com/photos/aura-chakra-yoga-meditation-5338110/

➤ Tumisu. (2019). Empathy and Compassion.

In Pixabay. https://pixabay.com/photos/empathy-compassion-friendship-4181896/